KANSAS CITY Scavenger

D1609612

Anne Kniggendorf
and Leslie Kniggendorf

Library of Congress Control Number: 2021950831

ISBN: 9781681063614

Cover and interior design by Claire Ford

Interior and front cover images courtesy of Anne Kniggendorf and Leslie Kniggendorf; interior clip art courtesy of Pixabay; back cover headshots courtesy of Chase Castor.

Printed in the United States of America
22 23 24 25 26 5 4 3 2 1

Dedication

For Fred and Rosemary Kniggendorf

We love you so much and are grateful
for all you do for our family.

Contents

Acknowledgments

Extra-special thanks to our Scavenger family helpers: Henry and Ellis Kniggendorf for driving around and hunting with Anne; Duane Cunningham for his incredible and unusual talent for enjambments (we had no idea!); and Arlo and Juniper Cunningham for their patience and riddle efforts.

We would also like to thank the following Scavenger friends for their invaluable help: Janet Casto and Jeremy Fowler, who endured unreasonably high temperatures for hours and hours, looking for just the right features to photograph. And Laura Evans for a lot: her editorial pass through the book, for tracking her children and Leslie's on "field trips" while Leslie took pictures, and for taking great notes.

Introduction

If you're holding this book, I don't need to give up any real estate to tell you about the scavenger hunt craze that's unfolding. It's big. And this book is the biggest collection of Kansas City clues you'll find anywhere.

Between the covers, you'll find more than 330 thumbnail photos and their corresponding rhyming riddles for 20 walkable areas around the metro. We tried to go light on stores and restaurants, times being what they are, but you'll still see a few. Mainly, though, this book will task you with hunting down murals, art installations, historic signs, architectural features, and oddball things like random letters in concrete, a coal chute, and canine hitching posts.

Now, before you say, "Hey, I see parts of town in the table of contents that are not actually in Kansas City," let me head you off. We're a much more inclusive city than that, aren't we? We are. Whether someone lives in Blue Springs or Shawnee, as these sisters do, we're all Kansas Citians, and this book is for everyone. Also, if we hadn't spread the wealth, how would you ever break out of your pandemic bubble and return to normal? This book is your ticket back.

For the most part, the areas we photographed and wrote about are pretty small, so if you're walking miles and miles on the outskirts of a neighborhood, turn back. The exception to this is the Crossroads—that's going to take some wandering—and, to a lesser extent, the financial/garment/library districts.

Yes, much of the poetry is bad. You could even say it's truly terrible and undeserving of the label "poetry." But . . . we laughed pretty hard writing it. Watch for new vocab words like "tintinnabulate"—new to Anne, anyway. And cut us some slack when you see a slant rhyme that's pretty much fallen completely over, like "Crossroads" and "aboard" or "herein" and "anything." How about "dinky" and "ink(y)"? Yeah. Some of these are rough.

We invite you to not only join us on this romp around the city you love, but also to write your own riddles—especially when you think ours are ridiculous. Hashtag #KansasCityScavenger on your favorite social media, or post to @kansascityscavenger on Instagram, and we'll see how well you do!

Now, throw on some weather-appropriate gear, lace up your sensible shoes, and join Anne and Leslie in looking a whole lot harder at your surroundings than you normally do.

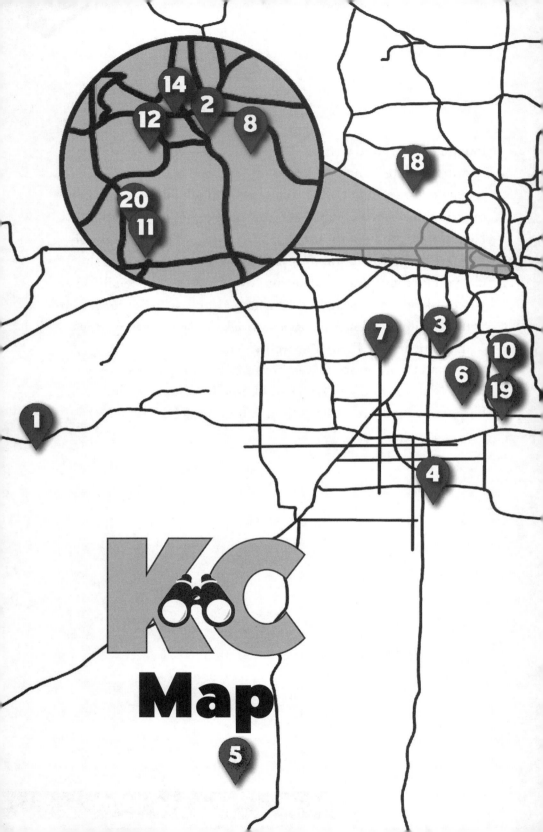

Legend

Kansas

1 Eudora

2 Kansas City

3 Mission

4 Old Overland Park

5 Paola

6 Prairie Village

7 Shawnee

Missouri

8 18th and Vine

9 Blue Springs

10 Brookside

11 Country Club Plaza

12 Crossroads

13 Excelsior Springs

14 Garment, Financial, and Library Districts

15 Harrisonville

16 Independence

17 Lee's Summit

18 Parkville

19 Waldo

20 Westport

Eudora

Eudora is a small town off of K-10 just east of Lawrence, Kansas, founded in 1857. You'll notice that many of the photos in this section are of signs. That's not typical of most neighborhoods in this book, but when we visited Eudora, many buildings were in disrepair or empty. Identifying features that wouldn't change in future remodels and rehabs was a challenge. In 2012, the city placed historical markers on nearly every building. In 2015, a historical museum opened on Main Street that sometimes offers walking tours.

1

It lets you know when to start and stop.
Often it sits on a building, up top.
Now you can ding it with your finger down low;
These days the clapper may just be for show.

2

You need it and farmers need it.
And grain goes up it, bit by bit.
It's big, and it's old
And sometimes it's even sold.

3

The name of the house is on the windmill.
You'll find it easily just up the hill.
Built in 1894,
It's a private residence; don't go to the door!

4

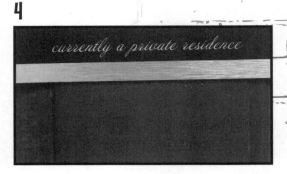

currently a private residence

Since 1896, this elegant ton of bricks
Has lived so many lives.
You may think you're out in the sticks,
But culture on this street thrives.

_____

_____

5

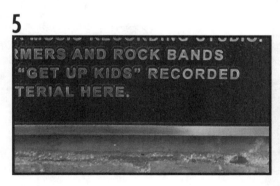

MERS AND ROCK BANDS
"GET UP KIDS" RECORDED
TERIAL HERE.

Going all the way back to the Civil War,
It's been much more than a grocery store.
If you want to make a beautiful tune
The setup here will make you swoon.

_____

_____

6

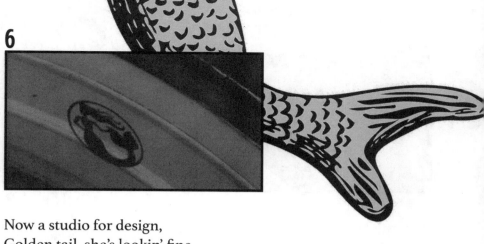

Now a studio for design,
Golden tail, she's lookin' fine.
She'd be no good to keep as a pet,
But you also don't want her in your net.

7

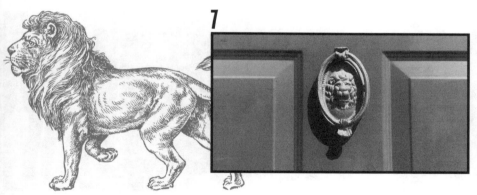

The door is blue, the fixtures brass;
Wouldn't want this creature on your a – – .
He found his courage in the land of Oz,
But, sadly, here he has no paws.

8

Its cornice, cupola, and cresting
Are impressive—and I'm not jesting.
Never empty for long, but it may be now,
The really cool paint job makes me say, "Wow!"

_____

_____

9

It's pretty much always been home to some fellows,
An international order that's known to be mellow.
They meet still on the second story,
Perhaps just like in their days of glory.

_____

_____

Kansas City Public Library
Central Library
14 West 10th Street
Kansas City, MO 64105.
816.701.3400

**Customer ID: **********3512

Items that you checked out

Title: Huda F are you?
ID: 00001893275505
Due: Monday, December 11, 2023
Messages:
Charged

Title: Kansas City scavenger
ID: 00001832966680
Due: Monday, December 11, 2023
Messages:
Charged

Title: Remote control
ID: 00001880326900
Due: Monday, December 11, 2023
Messages:
Charged

Total items: 3
Account balance: $0.00
11/20/2023 12:56 PM
Checked out: 3
Overdue: 0
Hold requests: 0
Ready for pickup: 0

Thank you

10

In its long, long life you'll find it has been
A place where much work's been undertaken.
Like undertaking (!), dry cleaning, orthocasts, and such,
But the longest-running tenants will get your pipes unstuck.

11

To make the mortar, the builder needed water,
So he scooped from the Wakarusa with his daughters.
From 1870 to 2007,
It helped to get people into heaven.

12

Along this street you can lose your favorite haunt,
But here, for a bit, it's been just one restaurant.
In the past you'd enter by a barber pole.
Now you go in for a hot egg roll.

_____

_____

13

All are welcome, not just the masons,
Every Dick, Rick, Tom, and Jason.
It's spacious and grand without being too much.
If you ask, you can bring your own cake, balloons, and such.

_____

_____

14

Find fun here in pieces and bits,
In cut-up squares and little kits.
Rose of Sharon, Pinwheel, or God's Eye;
They'll help you make whatever you try.

_____

_____

15

Its name you know as part of three;
Peter, ___, and good ol' Mary.
It's made of brick, strong and tall,
And called by a saint whose name is ___.

_____

_____

16

Meat market, meat market, where are you now?
Where shall I go to slaughter this cow?
You've sold many cuts upon this street;
Now, modern day, it's not about meat.

_____

_____

17

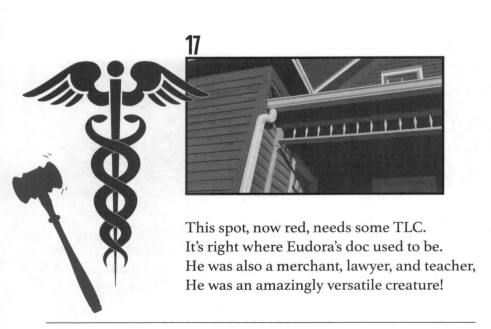

This spot, now red, needs some TLC.
It's right where Eudora's doc used to be.
He was also a merchant, lawyer, and teacher,
He was an amazingly versatile creature!

_____

_____

18

You'd guess this is a firehouse door
That's taken a most severe beating.
But when you look longer to try to learn more,
You'll find your understanding is fleeting.

_____

_____

19

He's got a nice hat and nubby arms;
His job's to extinguish dangerous harms.
Made in Alabama in 2008,
If you know you'll need him, you'd better not wait.

_____

_____

Kansas City

Kansas City was incorporated in 1886, and is the third-largest city in the state. The area you'll explore is the old downtown section, mostly along Minnesota Avenue. This neighborhood is diverse and rich in public art and history. We found that the older an area is, the easier it was to spot places of interest we could pass along to you.

1

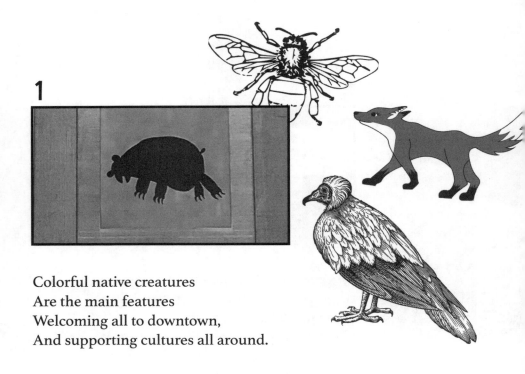

Colorful native creatures
Are the main features
Welcoming all to downtown,
And supporting cultures all around.

2

Upon a building very tall
Stands a symbol representing all
The workers who so long ago
Built the ironworks we now know.

_____

_____

3

A riot of dancing and colors await
The Dance of Life, a whirl of lace.
Here, traditions are displayed
And family love artfully conveyed.

_____

_____

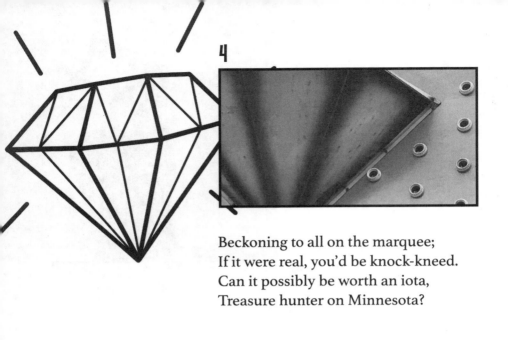

4

Beckoning to all on the marquee;
If it were real, you'd be knock-kneed.
Can it possibly be worth an iota,
Treasure hunter on Minnesota?

_____

_____

5

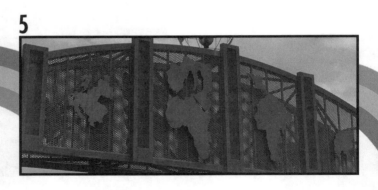

Spanning the street as you come or go,
The world overhead for all to know.
The city is warm and welcoming
To all visitors entering and exiting.

_____

_____

6

A historic and sacred location.
The resting place of a Nation.
It may have a strong snap;
The world was created on its back.

_____

_____

7

It's no "paper tiger" as you might think,
But a lion that used to guard the ink.
He roars on a building that shows the identity
Of the respected paper that serves the community.

_____

_____

8

Look across the parking lots to follow these clues
And find a building where they print the news.
Many a strong arm worked the press,
They're silent now, but online, no less.

_____

_____

9

Originally intended to advertise,
This beautiful item was installed streetside.
Since '15 it's graced Minnesota Avenue;
Now you can admire it from the bus queue.

_____

_____

10

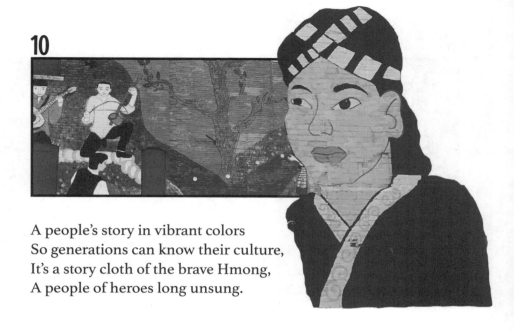

A people's story in vibrant colors
So generations can know their culture,
It's a story cloth of the brave Hmong,
A people of heroes long unsung.

11

Found on the corner for all to see
Is a department with great responsibility.
It's the HQ of those who will be hasty
To answer the call to protect your safety.

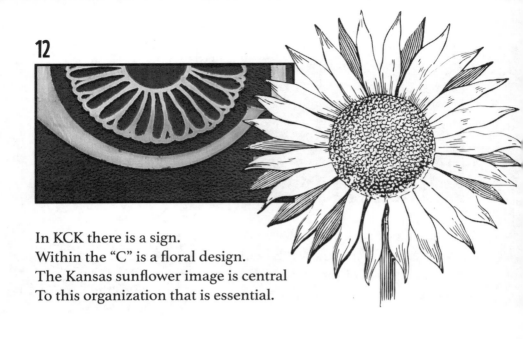

12

In KCK there is a sign.
Within the "C" is a floral design.
The Kansas sunflower image is central
To this organization that is essential.

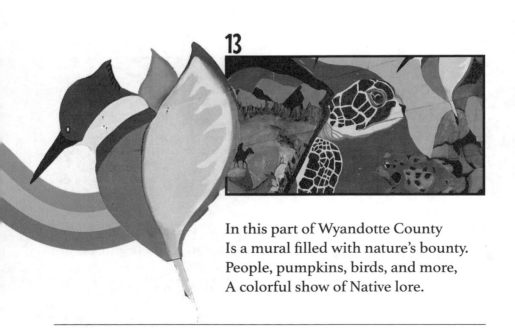

13

In this part of Wyandotte County
Is a mural filled with nature's bounty.
People, pumpkins, birds, and more,
A colorful show of Native lore.

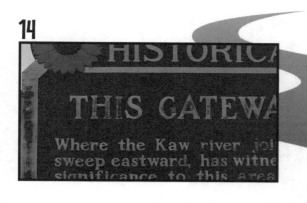

How to get to Kansas's glory?
Lots of history happened here.
Find this and you'll learn the story
'Cause this marker makes it clear.

_____

_____

KANSAS

Mission

From 1825 to 1854, what now is Johnson County officially belonged to the Shawnee Tribe thanks to a deal with the government. In 1854, the deal was scrapped, and the government opened the area to white settlers. The city of Mission was not incorporated until 1951. Its long downtown strip on Johnson Drive is lined with great local shopping and restaurants. You'll explore from Reeds Road to Lamar Avenue.

1

Along Johnson Drive are lots of tiny shops,
To find this place, study the tops.
Look for the diamond made of brick;
Come inside for a pastry, quick!

2

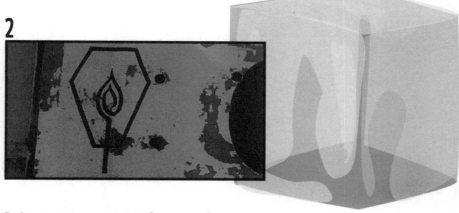

Is it rusty or rustic? Whatever the case,
It's neat to see on the side of this space.
Large black letters ringed by holes so small.
White paint's peeling on the sign of this, a strip mall.

3

Affixed to this wall where dancing goes down
Is a sign for a man who was loved in this town.
A plaque on this building holds his memory;
When you see it, stop; say hello to his tree.

4

A little place to see movies in 1938,
A charming little spot one might take his or her date.
These days you cannot view classic films here,
But can rent the space to marry your dear.

_____

_____

5

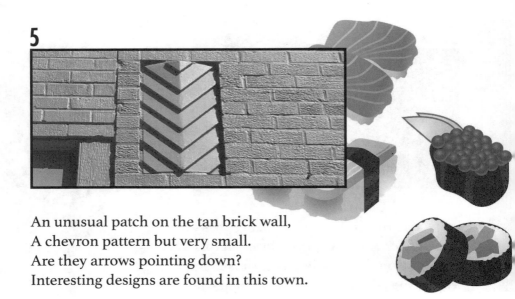

An unusual patch on the tan brick wall,
A chevron pattern but very small.
Are they arrows pointing down?
Interesting designs are found in this town.

_____

_____

6

Standing tall, it gives you the time of day;
Look at its face and it tells you the city.
You'll see a yellow cog on display;
Grab a donut next door and you'll be sitting pretty.

7

Set inside the stone foundations,
Find these fancy decorations.
Like four-leaf clovers inside rings.
I wonder what they call these things?

8

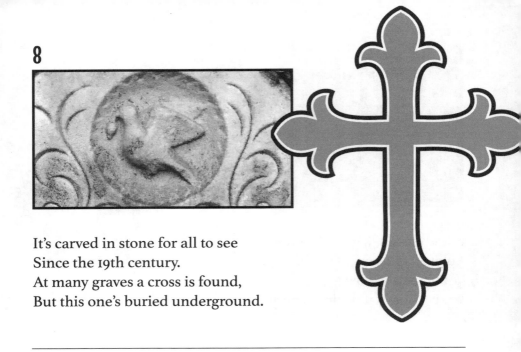

It's carved in stone for all to see
Since the 19th century.
At many graves a cross is found,
But this one's buried underground.

_____

_____

9

Find the spigot coming out
Of artwork made of tile and grout.
'Round a corner's where you'll find it,
With a building right behind it.

_____

_____

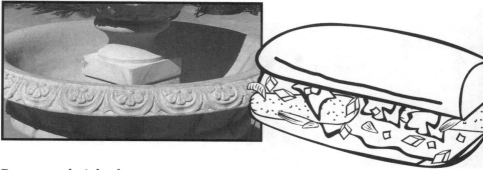

Buy a sandwich, then you go
To sit out on the patio.
Watch the fountain do its thing
And listen to the birds that sing.

_____

_____

KANSAS

Old Overland Park

A couple blocks off of Metcalf Avenue in northern Johnson County, the blocks around the clock tower were simply Overland Park for decades—without the words "old," "downtown," or "historic" in front of it. The area's roots go back to about 1905, but the city was not incorporated until 1960. In the 1990s, the location you're in right now was retooled to be what it is today: a great place to spend a chunk of your day looking at local shops and eating in local restaurants. Fun fact: Overland Park is the second-largest city in Kansas, behind Wichita.

1

View this item from afar.
Use CAUTION—don't get hit by a car!
This person envisioned a train line
And purchased land for this city, so fine.

_____

_____

2

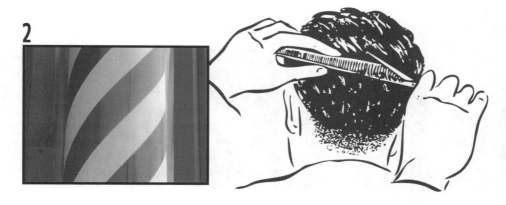

In days of old, we are told,
The barber was a surgeon.
Don't think of that when scheduling
A haircutting excursion!

_____

_____

3

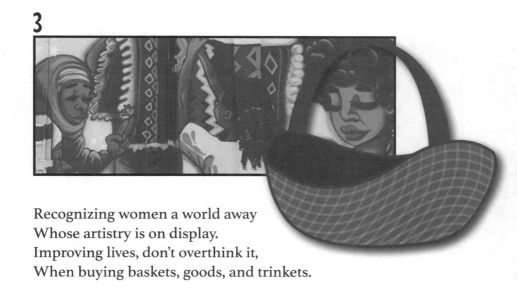

Recognizing women a world away
Whose artistry is on display.
Improving lives, don't overthink it,
When buying baskets, goods, and trinkets.

_____

_____

4

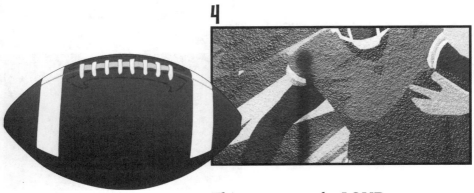

This represents the LOUD
And the proud.
Not in red, white, and blue,
But in KC colors—true.

5

Spring blooms abound,
Bees buzz around.
Earth welcomes gently
Good luck and prosperity.

6

Here, where tradition meets history,
The building's origins are no mystery.
A railroad line was the perfect entity
For developing the OP community.

7

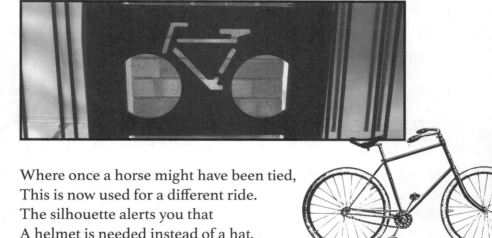

Where once a horse might have been tied,
This is now used for a different ride.
The silhouette alerts you that
A helmet is needed instead of a hat.

8

Need a break from all that shopping?
My, the businesses sure are hopping!
Stop and sit for a little while,
Inviting respite on colorful tile.

_____

_____

9

This is a place where two trails met.
Did you know this once was how to get
From Westport on to Santa Fe
Like brave families and traders of yesterday?

_____

_____

10

Do you see what she sees in the sky?
Migrating geese are passing by.
Sunflowers harvested in the afternoon,
Nature is blossoming and in tune.

11

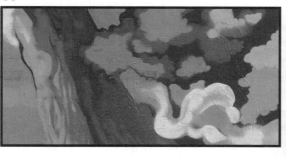

One of four artistic units
Described herein through hints
Evoking thoughts of home,
Where the clock strikes and shoppers roam.

12

Where what once was old now is new,
An upper-level space with a view.
The new brick building was destined
To have a name that lives up to the legend.

_____

_____

13

Well, "shoot," what can it be?
Look down, and you will see.
This relic of iron unfolds,
What's inside warded off the cold.

_____

_____

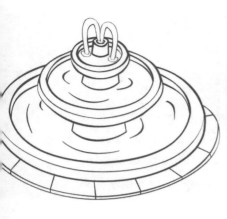

14

The fountain sprays,
Music and children play;
The clock tower's murals of unity
Depict values of the community.

15

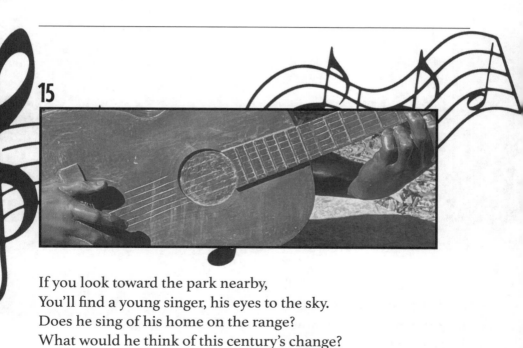

If you look toward the park nearby,
You'll find a young singer, his eyes to the sky.
Does he sing of his home on the range?
What would he think of this century's change?

Paola

Paola is Miami County's seat. The city website traces its history to the Native Americans who originally lived there, then to 1541, when Francisco Vázquez de Coronado came to town. In 1673, French Jesuit missionary explorers arrived. The city plat was laid out in 1855. The town's pride in its diversity is evident everywhere, but particularly in its square.

Heavy, curved, and made of metal,
If it were a drum, it'd be a kettle.
At 400 pounds its tone was right
To awaken the helpers to battle at night.

2

When you donate something here in this town,
Your friends will want to remember,
Maybe by placing a brick in the ground.
You'll see, when extinguishing an ember.

3

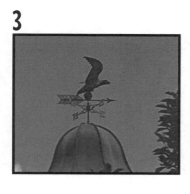

It's a wee metal bird, so look to the sky;
Sadly, it spins and cannot fly.
While you're there, take out some money;
Say this aloud, and it's sort of funny.

4

Right by where the brickwork ends,
Find answers about how the town began.
You can't wear the hat or even reach it,
But if it's a fact you want, these folks will teach it.

_____

_____

5

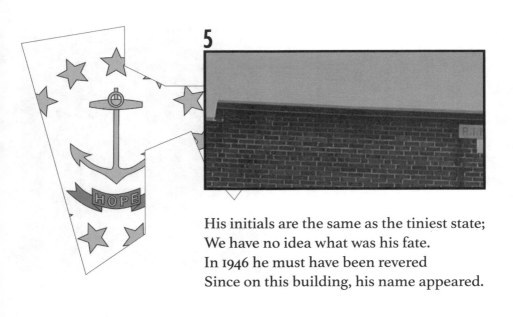

His initials are the same as the tiniest state;
We have no idea what was his fate.
In 1946 he must have been revered
Since on this building, his name appeared.

_____

_____

6

This photo of a clerk who is no more
Is sweet and sentimental town décor.
Find her face beneath a bell;
For Jill's life it will solemnly knell.

_____

_____

7

They are no "Patience" and "Fortitude,"
Yet here they perch, full of attitude.
Come on by and take a look
And while you're here, read a book.

_____

_____

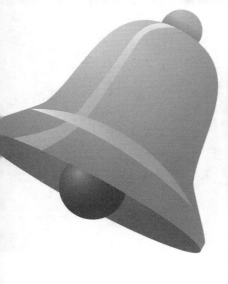

8

Inside this structure are some folks
Who probably wear hard-luck yokes.
Maybe their problems will be taken care of
And they'll start living "Ad Astra Per Aspera."

_____

_____

9

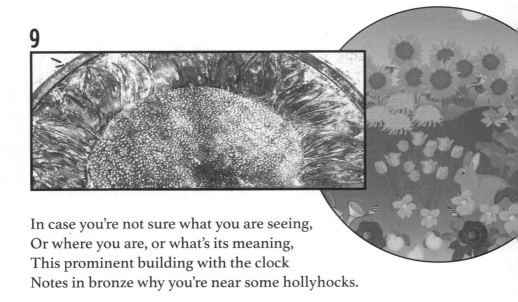

In case you're not sure what you are seeing,
Or where you are, or what's its meaning,
This prominent building with the clock
Notes in bronze why you're near some hollyhocks.

_____

_____

10

Next door to the courthouse sits
A lovely building made of bricks.
Find here a blessing, God, or peace;
Most parts of town see the cross with ease.

_____

_____

11

There's more than one bell in this old town,
When they all tintinnabulate, it's hard to frown!
Here's one up high, another down low.
This one gets used—it's not just for show.

_____

_____

12

Only one Kansas county is named for a woman,
You'll trip on her name when through the square you're a roamin'.
She was a nurse and a hero, but not a boss;
When needed, she stepped up to found the Red Cross.

_____

_____

13

From the base at Fort Hays, he went to the war
And was just 21 when he died.
His family and friends saw John no more
And oh, how his mother cried.

_____

_____

14

If you ask the Paolans about Jill
They'd likely call her a pretty big deal.
Only two memorials to her would be fair;
Find this one out in the town square.

15

Clarence was not from Paola, but Beagle;
It's said he proudly wore his eagle.
He died at Fort Riley, not off in France.
At just 21, he never had a chance.

16

Before the end of World War I
This statue was raised by daughters and sons
For 52 years, we know, 'cause it's dated,
Though the monument was never dedicated.

_____

_____

17

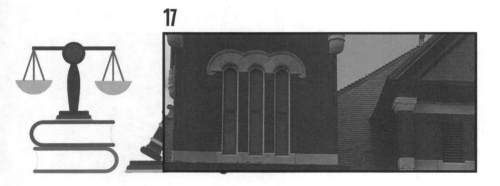

George Washburn designed 13 of these;
The one in Paola is sure to please.
With Carthage limestone for the foundation,
It's a standout building anywhere in the nation.

_____

_____

18

This husband and wife calmed many a strife,
Fostering diversity and cooperation;
As a couple and singly, they devoted their lives
To guide, care, and lead with patience.

19

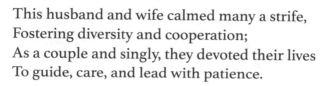

Birds don't often wear saddles,
Nor do children sit on their backs.
You'll go round and round when you straddle
These creatures and probably laugh.

Prairie Village

Prairie Village has several neighborhoods within it, but the one we walked was around 71st Street and Mission Road—the area we grew up visiting every week for music lessons. This section is store- and restaurant-heavy, for sure, but you'll find some good art and architectural features as well. The roots of the town go back to the Osage, Shawnee, and Kanza, but eventually ended up in the hands of developer J. C. Nichols.

1

This colorful mural is here to behold,
Depicting a family's journey of old.
They traveled the prairie and created their home,
At least for a while, no more to roam.

2

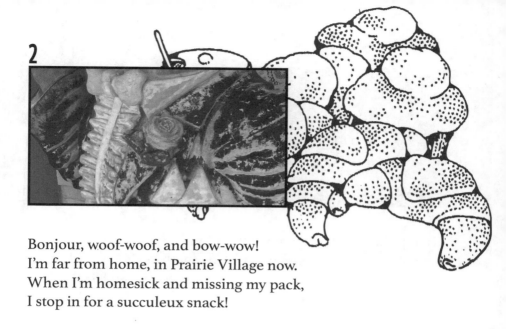

Bonjour, woof-woof, and bow-wow!
I'm far from home, in Prairie Village now.
When I'm homesick and missing my pack,
I stop in for a succuleux snack!

_____

_____

3

A symbol that means hospitality,
This one is unusually wet.
They don't grow on trees or even a bush,
But sweet and spiny? You bet!

_____

_____

4

This Republican was mayor when the Village was new,
Young couples moved here to raise up their broods.
New suburb, nice homes, yards with dogs that would bark,
Many years later, this dude has his own park!

_____

_____

5

No head, no legs, no arms—what's this?
This beauty in stone doesn't need them.
Tucked away in this park, it's not amiss,
As many stop by to see him.

_____

_____

6

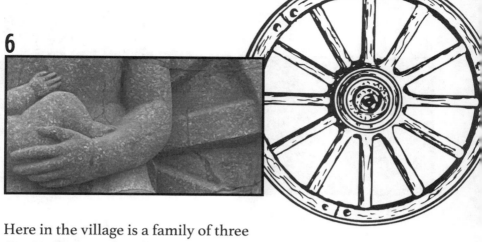

Here in the village is a family of three
Out in the open for all to see,
They never can leave, 'cuz here is the deal:
Their wagon is gone—all that's left is a wheel.

_____

_____

7

Wrestling angels or fighting nymphs?
These four pasty babies are wild.
Hairpulling and screaming—what got into these imps?
I know one thing: these children are riled.

_____

_____

8

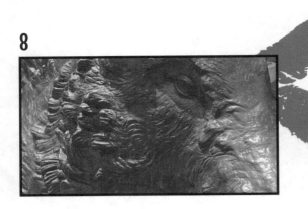

Out on the mall, he's cold and he's brown,
And he's got the shiniest nose in this town.
Some say a schnoz rub could bring you good luck,
But don't kiss him in winter or your lips will get stuck.

_____

_____

9

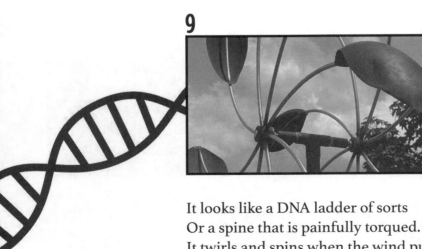

It looks like a DNA ladder of sorts
Or a spine that is painfully torqued.
It twirls and spins when the wind pushes.
A wind chime with no sound, only shushes.

_____

_____

10

On a square within a circle stands
A form made by an artist's hands.
On the brightest day, it stands there, gleaming,
Revealing what your mind is dreaming.

11

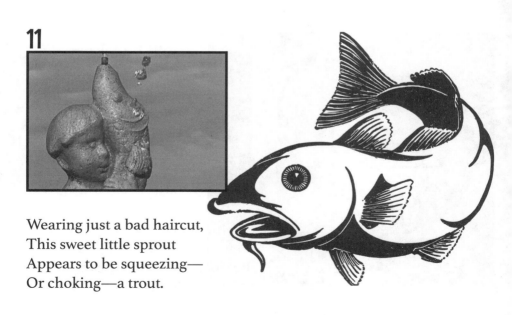

Wearing just a bad haircut,
This sweet little sprout
Appears to be squeezing—
Or choking—a trout.

KANSAS

Shawnee

The city of Shawnee was first called Gum Springs, back in 1856. In 1922, it took the name of the Indigenous people who lived there. For many decades, the area you'll explore around the intersection of Nieman Road and Johnson Drive looked pretty rough. Now, thanks to a neighborhood revitalization fund and some tax incentives, the old 'hood is shaping up. Here, you'll find a few murals, a little art, and several cool, old buildings.

1

If Chicken Little had her say
She'd be well-fed every day,
But long ago the cows came home
And now the sign is all alone.

_____

_____

2

This 1920s Shawnee anchor and venue
Sat empty for years as we patiently waited.
Revived with a new theatrical menu,
Its opening was highly anticipated.

_____

_____

3

Stones and rock, cathedrals and more,
This particular one's number is 54.
What happens within these mysterious walls?
Only their members are allowed in these halls.

_____

_____

4

Across from a brewery and near City Hall
With sparkling water enjoyed by all.
Green for St. Patrick's Day and even more,
Come by to explore what else is in store.

5

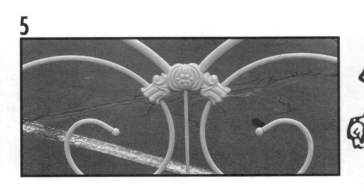

This childhood favorite's both repair shop and store
And is filled to the ceiling with keepsakes galore.
Memories are made, restored, and created;
The child in you will be thrilled and elated.

6

Over 84 years and still going strong,
They've checked out your car to find out what's wrong.
Walk past this trusted business landmark
And find downtown Shawnee's newest park.

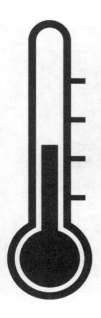

7

The bricks are bold in a bright tableau,
Are you too hot or cold? Let them know!
You should service your furnace before the first snow;
By summer your A/C will be ready to blow!

8

For 70 years we were there for you
To fix a mower or find a screw.
We may be gone, but don't despair,
Look 'round the corner; the "boy" is still there.

_____

_____

9

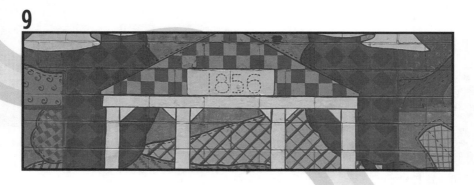

In Shawnee a historian painted a mural
Depicting the city from when it was rural.
It looks like a quilt and it's there on a wall
Where it can be seen and admired by all.

_____

_____

10

Pretend rolling hills with holes to explore,
A spherical structure to climb,
Stepping stones and ropes galore,
A place to play and spend some time.

_____

_____

11

A favorite spot in any weather
For families and friends to get together.
Round, hot, fresh, and hearty,
Being here always feels like a party.

_____

_____

12

REOPENED
EAR 2065

In the lawn of City Hall it's buried deep;
You can walk by or drive past at a creep.
But what's inside? It's years 'til we learn;
In the meantime, our curiosity must burn.

13

Shawneetown was once corralled
By Quantrill's Raiders on the prowl.
Though looted and burned in a violent spree,
Kansas prevailed and the state remained free!

14

Enter this peaceful and comforting home
Through three of the same, but not a dome.
A yellow rose is displayed, a welcoming beckon
To bring you peace at a time of reflection.

15

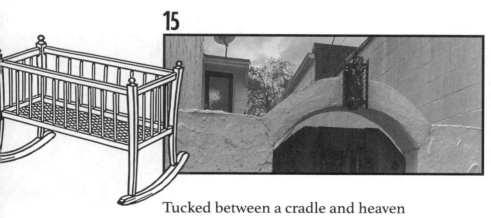

Tucked between a cradle and heaven
Across from where once sat a 7-Eleven
Is a wooden door with no window, high walls.
What'll you find? Maybe more broken dolls?

16

Nearly 100 years ago,
Wearing a banner to bestow
Good health and body strong,
Lifted wings but not in song.

17

In a wagon procession
With all their possessions,
They farmed the land
Where the city still stands.

Luxury living in Shawnee's downtown,
Standing tall right off of Nieman with a bright blue crown.
You can walk to and from all of the cool little shops
And stop next door for the best pizza and hops.

_____

_____

18th and Vine

For decades during the 20th century, redlining forced Black Kansas Citians to stay south of 27th Street, so the neighborhood of 18th and Vine Streets became a hub of Black businesses and the arts. Now, it's home to many historic buildings, the American Jazz Museum, the Negro Leagues Baseball Museum, the Kansas City Urban Youth Academy, restaurants, shops, and a lot of art. The area continues to change and grow and is a source of pride for all Kansas Citians.

1

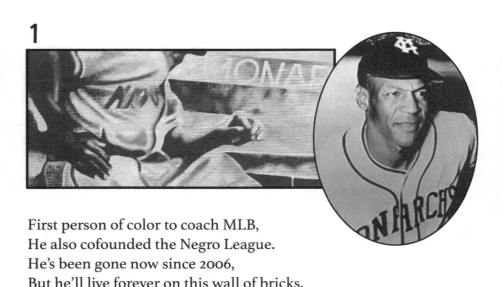

First person of color to coach MLB,
He also cofounded the Negro League.
He's been gone now since 2006,
But he'll live forever on this wall of bricks.

2

Smiling people in the stands,
A baseball bat rests in his hands,
Jackie Robinson and Satchel Paige;
In this spot, they'll never age.

3

It's a family heirloom and national treasure,
For decades providing musical pleasure.
The art born in NOLA was honed in KC;
This neon sign in the night sky is something to see.

Known throughout the world for its sound,
In this blue place it can be found.
It's not just a venue, but a proper club:
Kansas Citians can be proud of this hub.

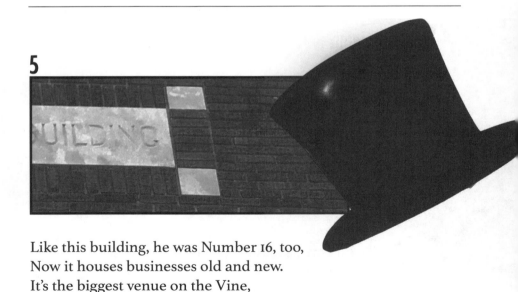

5

Like this building, he was Number 16, too,
Now it houses businesses old and new.
It's the biggest venue on the Vine,
Hopping with activity all the time.

6

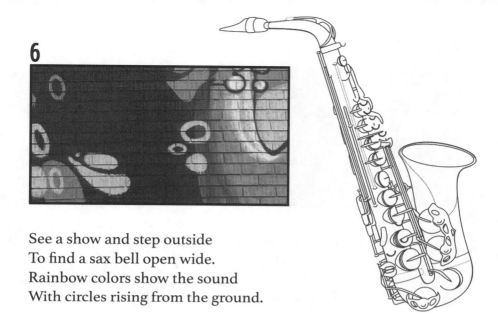

See a show and step outside
To find a sax bell open wide.
Rainbow colors show the sound
With circles rising from the ground.

_____

_____

7

Kansas City honored this great musician
Who led the orchestra, in addition.
It's been 80 years since he's passed;
Now his name in bronze is cast.

_____

_____

8

He was born on the Kansas side
And was only 34 when he died.
A favorite son he became,
Early inductee to the Walk of Fame.

9

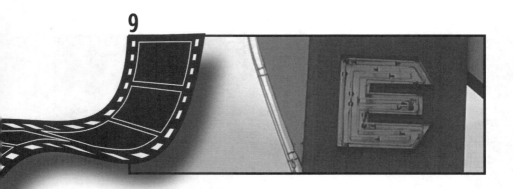

Once a silent movie palace,
Its name is an object on a royal chalice.
In 1912 built with horses and carts,
Now it stands as a center of arts.

10

Fans flock to it from across the sea
To bask not only in the creativity
But also in the sights, sounds, and history
Of an era that's still important and always will be.

_____

_____

11

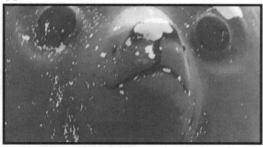

Near the stairs, decked out in a tux,
It looks like he could use a few bucks.
Musical notes climb up his sleeves;
In the fall—poor guy—he's covered in leaves.

_____

_____

12

All manner of people are cut from steel—
They hop, walk, play, and run.
You'll be dazzled by its shimmery appeal,
Especially when you stand in the sun.

13

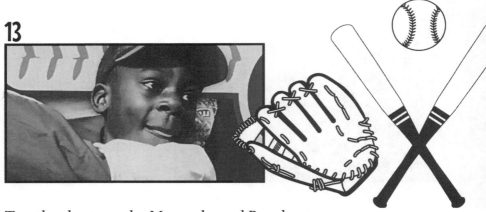

Together here are the Monarchs and Royals,
Surrounded by children's playful toils.
They run their hardest and swing their bats,
And, for the most part, wear matching hats.

14

In the center of the diamond, the ball wears a crown.
You can almost hear the cheering sound
Of those who admire the youthful athletes,
Sliding into home in their tiny cleats.

_____

_____

15

It's a jumping joint with chicken and waffles;
Try it out when you've got "the awfuls."
There's karaoke, dancing, and soul sessions, too,
And blues and jazz when you're feeling . . . blue.

_____

_____

16

They're old-school barbers, red, white, and blue,
They'll color, trim, and razor-cut, too.
Head to the jazz district if you're feeling plain;
It's probably just time for a change to your mane.

17

Chester Franklin saw a need and issued a call;
Quality info is a necessity for all.
From 1919 to the present
This news has been reliable and intelligent.

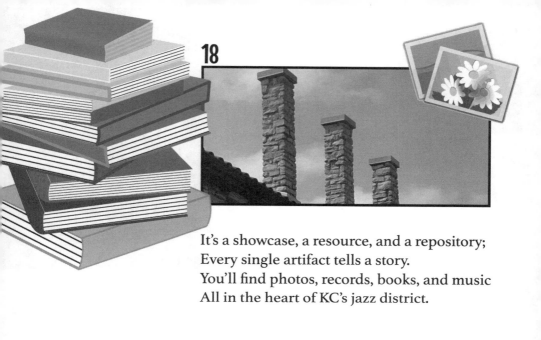

18

It's a showcase, a resource, and a repository;
Every single artifact tells a story.
You'll find photos, records, books, and music
All in the heart of KC's jazz district.

_____

_____

19

Editor of *The Crisis* just after Du Bois,
Of the civil rights movement he was "senior statesman."
In writing and justice he found many joys
And fought for equity of life for each human.

_____

_____

20

In 1912, it was "Parks and Boulevards"
And needed an operating plant that was quite large.
It housed maintenance and storage till 2003;
Now it's something else entirely.

_____

_____

21

This concrete slab isn't a grand memorial,
But flowers are placed in a way that's ceremonial.
Don't ever forget our lost veterans,
Not even when you're parking to do errands.

_____

_____

22

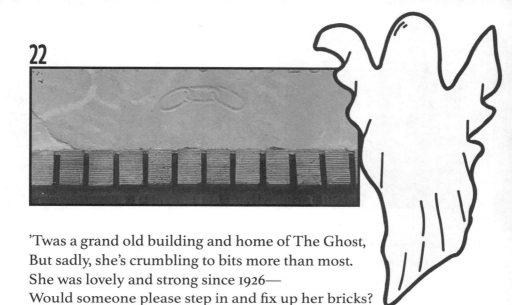

'Twas a grand old building and home of The Ghost,
But sadly, she's crumbling to bits more than most.
She was lovely and strong since 1926—
Would someone please step in and fix up her bricks?

23

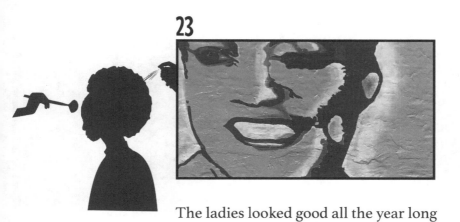

The ladies looked good all the year long
Back then, when this was a hair salon.
For many years it's been empty and forlorn.
Now open, we're glad, with her face it's adorned.

24

Developers say they were built to last
But rebuilding for reuse has not been fast.
It was KC's first public works facility;
Now it's on its way to hip and pretty.

25

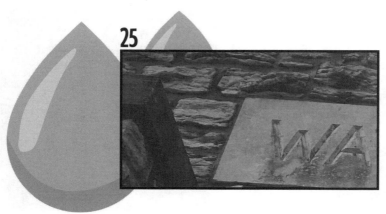

Since 1866, this limestone structure's stood here,
Once used for utilities, that job won't reappear.
Looking good now under its original sign,
This whole part of town is doing just fine.

26

Created by sculptor Robert Graham,
Find the bust of this important man.
The jazziest sound you've ever heard
Came from the sax of this big Bird.

_____

_____

Blue Springs

This town attracted pioneers migrating west because of its supplies of fresh water. A spring of the Little Blue River inspired the name Blue Springs, and the town was first incorporated in 1880. In its old downtown, you'll find a lot of art, some good local shops and restaurants, and a few surprising details that would be easy to walk right by unless you were hunting for them.

1

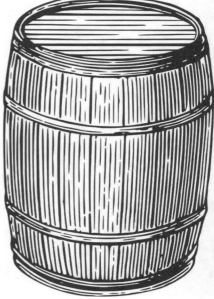

Strolling past The Keg dive bar,
This pictured item can't be far.
Look up, look up—No, wait, look down!
The world's shortest parade was here in town.

_____

_____

2

Passing by this lovely home
Stands a horse that cannot roam.
This trusty, rusty steed of steel
Proudly stands on wagon wheels.

3

Two blooms glisten in the sun,
A stem of steel for each one.
At Tenth and Main, it sure is handy
To come across these flowers so dandy.

4

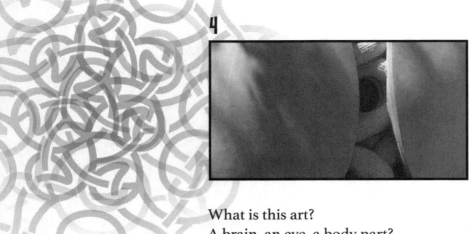

What is this art?
A brain, an eye, a body part?
Is it watching? Is it growing?
Never mind, let's just keep going.

_____

_____

5

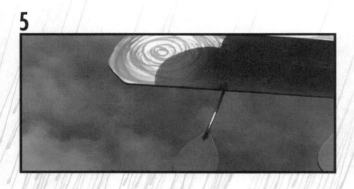

An old water tower
Yields a cloud and rain shower.
It moves in the breeze
To enjoy as you please.

_____

_____

6

It's tall and red and OH so happy.
Festooned with ribbons, it looks so snappy.
Right there by a parking lot,
You're sure to find—it's easy to spot!

_____

_____

7

Take a stroll on down Main Street
To a building where men meet.
This pictured item's above the door,
But what it says is there no more.

_____

_____

8

These bricks, painted so colorfully,
Depict Blue Springs historically.
Welcome to our quaint downtown!
Come on by and look around.

9

Such a teeny, tiny spot
In such a teeny, tiny lot.
This big fella in the yard
Stands and gazes ever skyward.

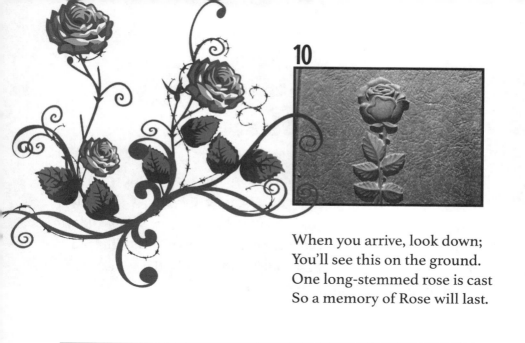

10

When you arrive, look down;
You'll see this on the ground.
One long-stemmed rose is cast
So a memory of Rose will last.

11

Look up high on the building's side.
Keep your peepers open wide.
Giant button, knob, or bling?
What the heck is this round thing?

Brookside was an area dedicated to shopping, years before the Country Club Plaza made that claim to fame, though J. C. Nichols designed both. Construction of the first stores began in 1919. Today, the area is home to around 90 businesses and many beautiful, old homes. When we walked these blocks, we stuck by the stores and restaurants and didn't stray into the neighborhoods.

1

Above a door and doorstep
In a place where business is kept,
There is some ancient-looking trim.
Could "old" money be within?

2

Grab your Nikon.
There's an icon,
On a yellow wall, to be admired,
Where "Parking Only" is required.

3

Like leaves blowing in the wind,
When they turn we can't pretend
To understand. So, enjoy the to-and-fro.
The spinning motion is the show.

4

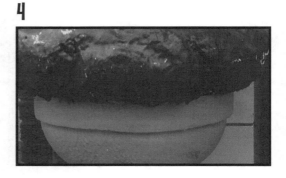

A trio of flavors
In giant-sized layers.
Please get some quick!
Lickety-split.

5

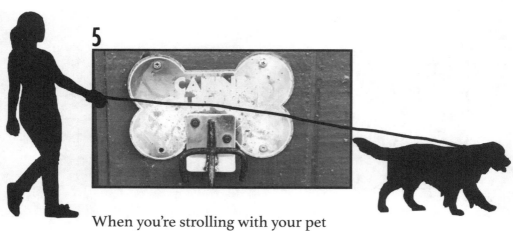

When you're strolling with your pet
And to your destination you get,
This will be handy while you're stopping
If your hands are full from shopping.

6

Find three lamps that do not glow
On a gate: they're just for show.
They give no light but match a trio
Standing on the corner below.

7

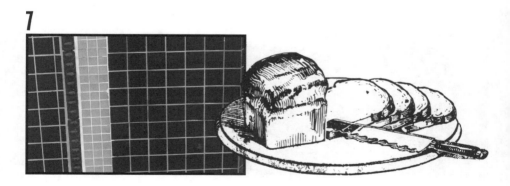

When you're at a stop sign red
By a place named for a bread
You may find yourself surprised
To see a corner glamorized.

8

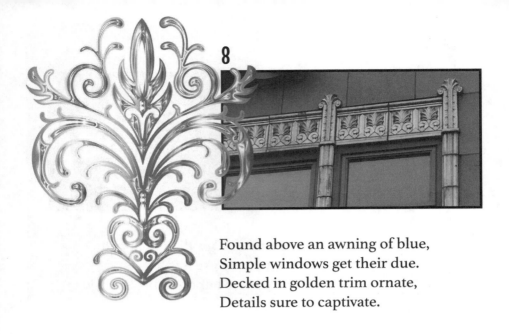

Found above an awning of blue,
Simple windows get their due.
Decked in golden trim ornate,
Details sure to captivate.

9

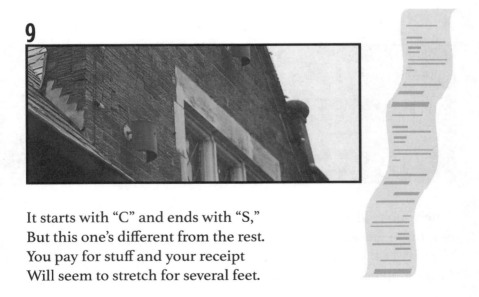

It starts with "C" and ends with "S,"
But this one's different from the rest.
You pay for stuff and your receipt
Will seem to stretch for several feet.

10

In Brookside, this is where you go
To buy a steaming cup of joe.
These coffee cups they hope you'll like;
They're here for you to park your bike.

11

Every picture on this wall
Relates to coffee, one and all.
People, dogs, and cats and pots
And drops of coffee—lots and lots!

12

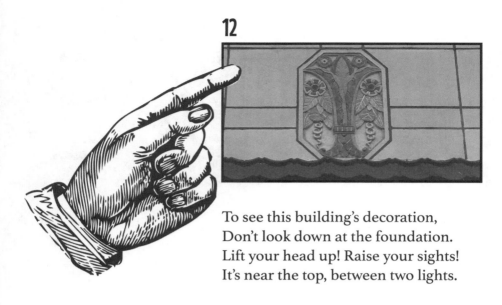

To see this building's decoration,
Don't look down at the foundation.
Lift your head up! Raise your sights!
It's near the top, between two lights.

13

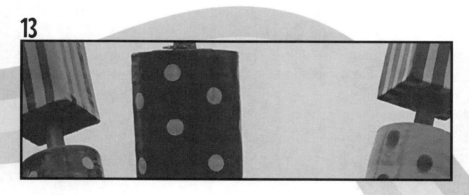

Colorful blocks on larger-than-life sticks
Dress up this corner with a childish fix.
Outside of a Brookside Montessori school,
Paul Storms's sculptures brightly rule.

14

The Earth is a classroom; here's an example,
This sign represents a fine, soily sample.
A place for kids to get out and explore.
'Cuz learning can totally take place outdoors.

15

Stamped here firmly in gray concrete,
It's so subtle and so discreet.
Someone has left their engraved mark
From 2001, so . . . not Lewis and Clark.

Country Club Plaza

Architect Edward Delk completed the plans for the Country Club Plaza in 1922. The district was the first shopping area in the nation designed specifically for people arriving by car. It's still one of the easiest places to park in Kansas City. The Spanish Revival style of the buildings, in addition to the fountains and mosaics, continues to make this a favorite place for locals to spend an afternoon strolling. Learn a few more details as you work to puzzle out these clues.

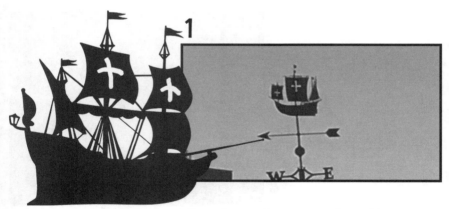

This ship sails on time, literally,
But might blow east, west, north, or southerly.
Beneath her, golden tiles gleam;
She's powered only by wind, never steam.

2

This ancient god is ruler of the sea
As well as his swimming horsies.
In 1911, English-made for a Philly estate,
Saved by Nichols from a scrap heap, before it was too late.

_____

_____

3

Above the Mexican president's fish,
And across from many an Italian dish,
The tiles take you to another land,
A woman walks, bulls work with a man.

_____

_____

4

He's an angry little man with a pageboy 'do
By a coat of arms and a lot of curlicues.
Appreciate his setting for being ornate;
Don't look him in the eye or give into his hate.

5

Mother and child, perched upon marble,
Maybe just before bed, maybe learning to gargle.
Don't make it weird, they're probably just talking;
You'll run into them soon, if you just keep walking.

6

Hey, horses, no fighting!
What's next, flat-toothed biting?
Save it for the movies, though maybe not here.
What'll go in next is really not clear.

_____

_____

7

Here's a bird far from Brush Creek;
You'd find her faster if she could speak.
Folks round here like lots of down,
What'd you expect in this part of town?

_____

_____

8

Might as well google "Conestoga Wagon"
So you'll know what you're seein'.
The marker celebrates a hundred years
and prominently features a couple of mule ears.

9

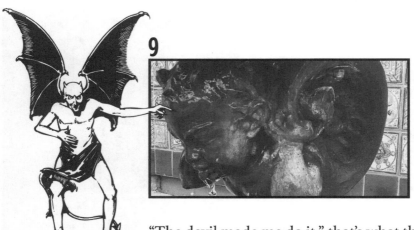

"The devil made me do it," that's what they all say,
But it might be true for this boy at play.
The devil's right there, not far from the frog,
And it's pretty hard to say who's going whole-hog.

10

Say hello on your way in for brunch;
I hope she didn't dump all the creamer!
Taunting with her bird and deep navel bunch,
Perhaps her sweet smile will redeem her.

11

It's sailed here since '92
And it rhymes with "ocean blue."
The ship's still cool, Columbus not so much;
The detail is great, let's say it's Dutch.

12

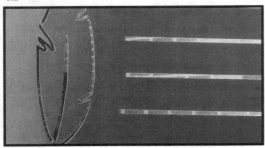

It could be a leaf, but it's probably a feather,
I'd bet that, inside, the seats are all pleather.
Haven't been in, it looks kinda pricey;
This sturdy wrought iron is anything but dicey.

_____

_____

13

High on a pole, with horns on his head,
His pinched little face says, "I wish you were dead."
He's up in the air and can't hurt you too bad,
Maybe you once caught a film here with dad.

_____

_____

14

The Nichols name has now been struck
From famed fountain, not from a duck.
If looking for clothes, they ain't got any,
But the whole dang thing is full of pennies.

_____

_____

15

Set back by a driveway, not up in an aerie,
Surrounded by windows, the nest must get scary.
The eaglets are crying out for their mom;
She'd better not leave, or else they'll be gone.

_____

_____

16

Way up high at the top of some stairs
Stands the gateway to the whole district.
That works for me, you, and your heirs
If your definition of "entrance" ain't too strict.

17

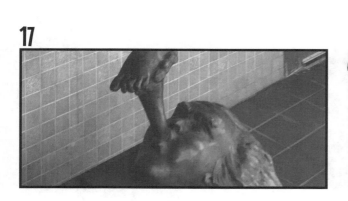

Don't put that winged foot in my mouth,
Unless I personify winds from the south.
With flying feet, are gusts really needed?
This god must be happiest when his message is speeded.

18

It's hard to say what will draw your sight
To this ornate iron post made for light.
You'll find serpents and steer hooves as well as dragons
Alongside eggs, fruit, and faces of lions.

_____

_____

19

Got a friend who thinks bullfights are cool?
Show them this triptych made in Seville.
It's no surprise the pictures are gory;
Try to put it in the form of a story.

_____

_____

20

Not far from the eagles with mom in the nest,
You'll notice a box with a small request.
Might be antique, not sure it's still valid,
Better be sure before you pull out your wallet.

_____

_____

21

Androgynous, naked figures ring
This big white urn where you enter parking.
Why is their stone hair all just the same?
It's impossible to say if they're playing a game.

_____

_____

22

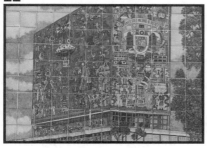

Near a lash studio in an alley
Stands a tribute to a university, that's really quite jolly.
See symbols, shapes, and picture surprises,
Then count how many stories this building rises.

_____

_____

MISSOURI

Crossroads

Let me tell you, Scavengers, this area was bigger than we initially imagined. The Crossroads's official boundary lines are from Broadway Boulevard to Oak Street and about 22nd Street to Interstate 670. Nearly a hundred years ago, the neighborhood was home to Film Row and acted as a central distribution point for companies like Paramount and Warner Brothers. When those businesses left, urban blight took hold. Over the past few decades, artists have worked to revitalize the area, which is now home to galleries, studios, living spaces, shops, and restaurants.

1

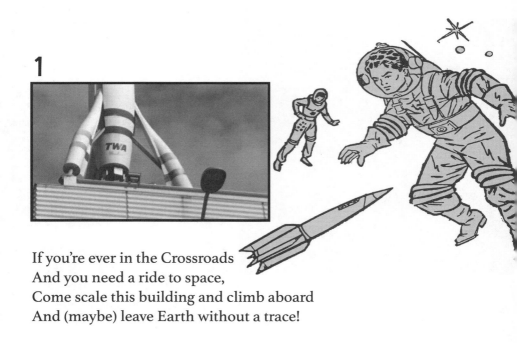

If you're ever in the Crossroads
And you need a ride to space,
Come scale this building and climb aboard
And (maybe) leave Earth without a trace!

2

This interesting symbol will catch your eye;
You will want to go in for a cocktail to try.
Named after the planet that is so tiny,
The starry cityscape view is equally shiny.

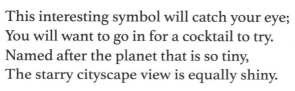

3

In 1905, this store was born,
Giving men the best wardrobe ever worn.
Suits, shoes, belts, and formal attire;
Only the finest for their buyer.

4

A bird of copper has made its nest
On this building that might put your beliefs to the test.
A religion begun by the youngest Eagle Scout.
Human spirit and the universe are what it's about.

_____

_____

5

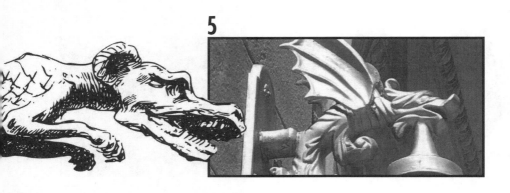

On a Gothic/modern building you will see
Interesting light fixtures fit its style to a tee.
Is it a dragon with an interesting growth?
A vomiting griffon? Or perhaps it's both?

_____

_____

6

Blue, green, and white paint on bricks
With an invaluable message that certainly sticks.
Be good to each other and kind to your peer.
Brave, strong, and bold, it's what women need to hear.

7

Convenience and luxury behind this cool tile,
A grand place to visit or stay for a while.
Head south to escape or north for great views,
Steps away, catch a ride to wherever you choose.

8

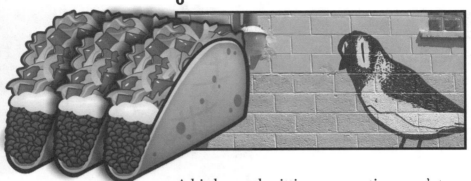

A bird sweetly sitting on a resting man's toes,
A bellyfull of some of KC's best tacos.
Graffiti by artist Alex Senna is pretty cool.
That dog is passed out; do you see any drool?

_____

_____

9

So . . . it's plantlike and green
With big, naked toes,
But what stands out most
Is the vine with the nose.

_____

_____

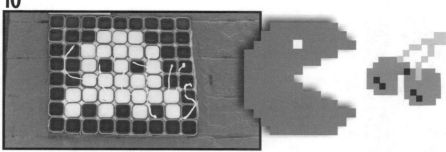

Trust them, it's art, there's no way around it,
Looks like a Pac-Man ghost (a tiny bit).
Blue and white with four legs so wee,
Doesn't matter what it is, 'cuz it's ART, ya see?

11

When you think of First Fridays you think of this sign
That's been hanging up there for quite a long time.
Yes, Opie sold brushes, but not the art type;
Rather, mops and brooms of every stripe.

12

Though the Crossroads 'hood has plenty of bars,
Only one has a squirrel gazing at stars.
A cool tavern with an original hook:
Sipping your booze whilst reading a book.

13

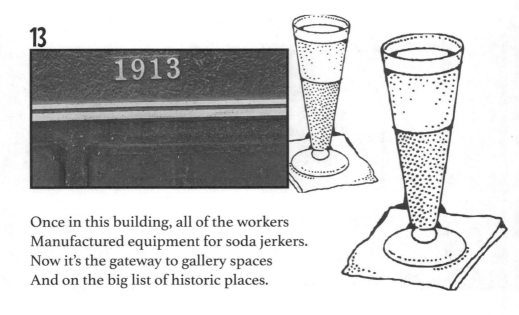

Once in this building, all of the workers
Manufactured equipment for soda jerkers.
Now it's the gateway to gallery spaces
And on the big list of historic places.

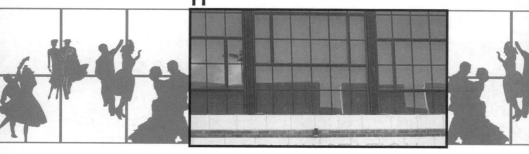

A classy old building from roof to the floor,
This is one doorway, although it has more.
Upscale is the restaurant, a crow on the wall,
A fancy event space on top of it all.

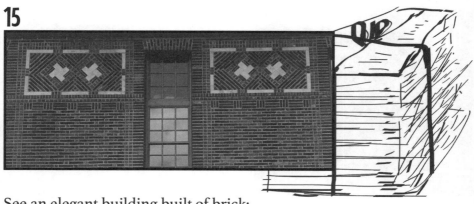

See an elegant building built of brick;
Details abound, wherever you pick.
Such as intricate patterns like herringbone tweed.
For decades it housed the *KC Star* that we read.

Excelsior Springs

Excelsior Springs was "Missouri's National Health Resort" from the discovery of its "healing" waters in 1880 until 1963. The whole town was founded on what Native Americans had known for centuries: the 40 types of mineral waters in the area have healing properties. Here, you'll scavenge the quaint downtown near the Hall of Waters. Go check that out, too, while you're in the neighborhood.

1

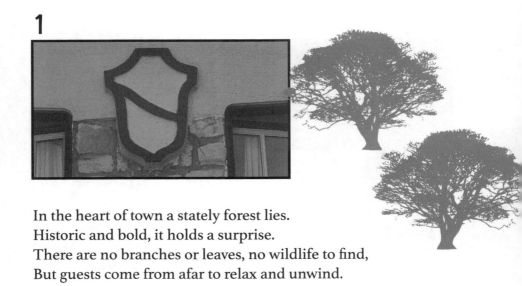

In the heart of town a stately forest lies.
Historic and bold, it holds a surprise.
There are no branches or leaves, no wildlife to find,
But guests come from afar to relax and unwind.

2

It's been around for many a year
And Patton was its engineer.
Use it so your feet stay dry;
It keeps you safe as cars go by.

_____

_____

3

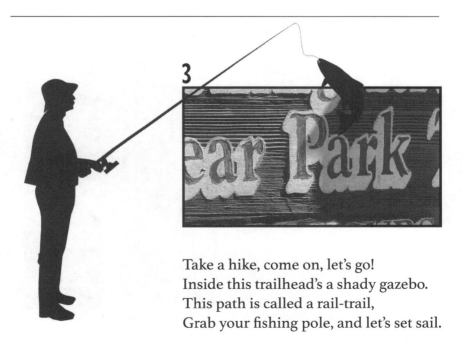

Take a hike, come on, let's go!
Inside this trailhead's a shady gazebo.
This path is called a rail-trail,
Grab your fishing pole, and let's set sail.

_____

_____

4

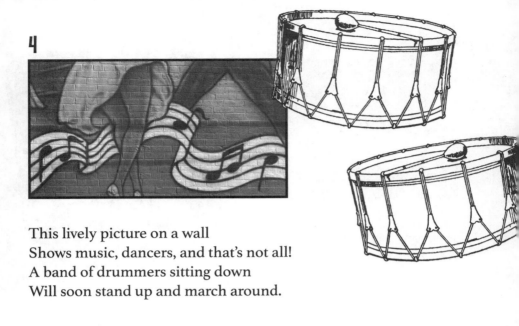

This lively picture on a wall
Shows music, dancers, and that's not all!
A band of drummers sitting down
Will soon stand up and march around.

_____

_____

5

The letters have faded
On this ancient brick,
What was once a garage
For when your car got sick.

_____

_____

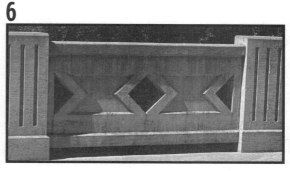

6

South of the rest of the list, just a smidge,
Is this beautiful, well-crafted Art Deco bridge,
A plaque for a congressman on the side,
Right next to a path for a pretty bike ride.

_____

_____

7

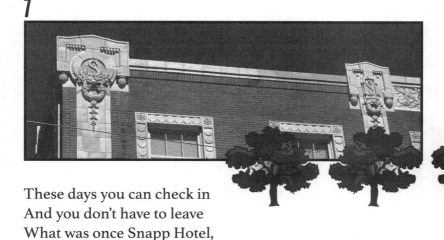

These days you can check in
And you don't have to leave
What was once Snapp Hotel,
A temporary reprieve.

_____

_____

8

You better not speed and you better not steal,
Or you may see a building all trimmed out in teal
With stylish square windows, right angles and lines,
Where the judge bangs a gavel and hands out the fines.

_____

_____

9

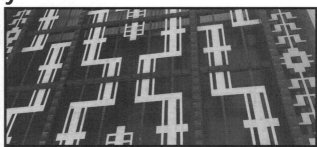

Will it bring you health, will it make you well?
Who's to say? There's no way to tell.
The Art Deco alone will draw a crowd;
A first of its kind, making Missourians proud.

_____

_____

10

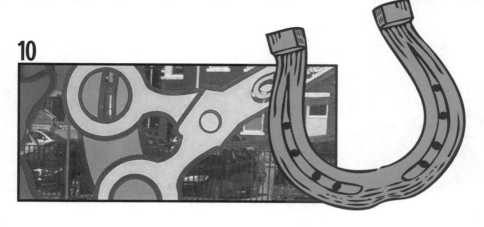

Get a clean fade, get a sharp line,
Get a nice trim right over on Cline.
If you need a hint, as you pass through,
Just look for the sign with the lucky horseshoe.

11

If you're seeking a place to take in a show,
I'll bet you love Broadway, but it's so far to go.
If you'll settle for Broadway that's "slightly" askew,
You're in luck! We've got just the place for you!

12

It's not every day that you get to dine
At a classic burger joint older than 89.
So check off your list when you see their sign,
And if you want fries, theirs are just fine.

_____

_____

13

If you can fly or jump really high,
Downtown's got a mysterious door you can try.
I actually suppose a ladder would do,
But that may disrupt a local business or two.

_____

_____

14

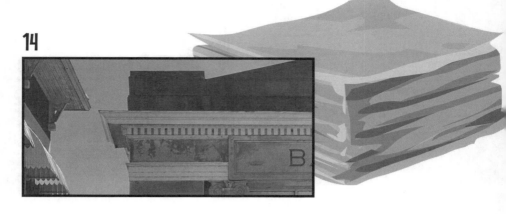

Known for its windows into the past
Where newspaper archives forever will last.
Excelsior Springs springs eternally here,
A lure for visitors both far and near.

_____

_____

15

Named after one of Excelsior Springs's mayors,
But that job's just one of her brightly colored layers.
This lady loved to travel, she went everywhere.
Check out the murals, as long as you're there.

_____

_____

16

Look upon this wall and see
A glimpse of how life used to be.
The horses are all saddled up
And guarded by a curious pup.

17

Blue and white, it makes a greeting,
Asking you to take a meeting.
It's a place to have some fun,
Established in 1881.

18

Just beyond this bright red door
You'll find walls so stoney.
Some worship, congregate, and more;
Some unite in matrimony.

_____

_____

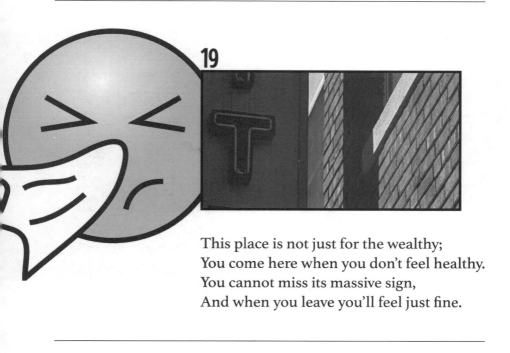

19

This place is not just for the wealthy;
You come here when you don't feel healthy.
You cannot miss its massive sign,
And when you leave you'll feel just fine.

_____

_____

Garment, Financial, and Library Districts

Scavengers, we want to be honest with you about something. We parked the car not far from the glorious Kansas City Public Library and just started walking, heedless of what districts we were entering and exiting. You're going to want to walk along Eighth, Ninth, and 10th streets, between about Broadway Boulevard and Walnut Street. Just wander around the way we did, and you'll find some of the most gorgeous architecture you could ever hope to see.

1

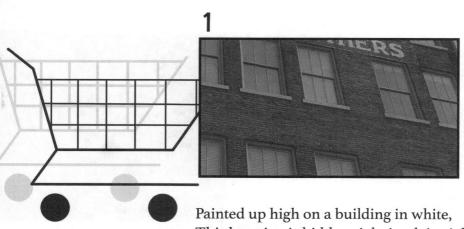

Painted up high on a building in white,
This lettering is hidden right in plain sight.
A place that once was dry goods storage
Now houses people in lofts for four stories.

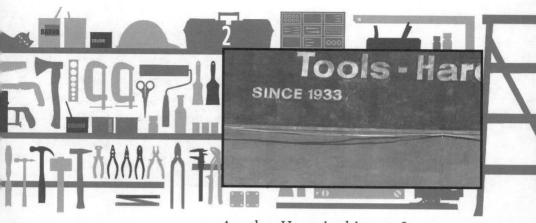

2

Another Harry in this town?
There's room enough to go around.
The decades-old company housed herein
Has tools to fix most anything!

3

Look above the canopy and find a surprise;
Two friendly, blue penguins stand and supervise
At a famous old hotel that only very recently
Was renewed and revived for the 21st century.

4

Slivers of colored glass in a pattern;
Do they evoke images of forests or lanterns?
Stained glass styles may come and go;
This window of yesteryear is Art Nouveau.

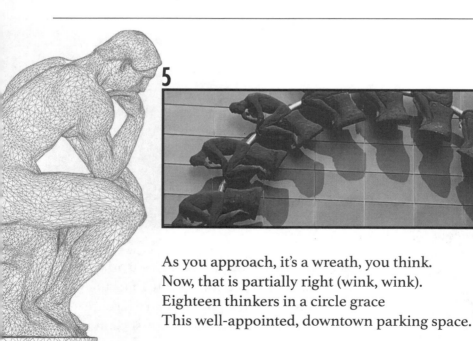

5

As you approach, it's a wreath, you think.
Now, that is partially right (wink, wink).
Eighteen thinkers in a circle grace
This well-appointed, downtown parking space.

6

He sits and watches passersby,
He loved to write, his wit was dry.
Sometimes funny, sometimes dark,
Looks like he's sitting in a park.

_____

_____

7

Three stories high and bricks of red,
Built in 1889, it is said,
In the High Victorian Italianate style.
Any "builder" or "trader" will certainly smile.

_____

_____

8

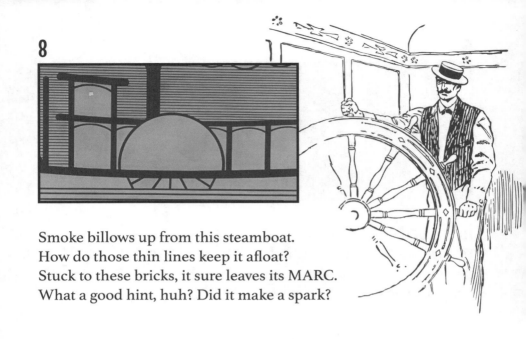

Smoke billows up from this steamboat.
How do those thin lines keep it afloat?
Stuck to these bricks, it sure leaves its MARC.
What a good hint, huh? Did it make a spark?

_____

9

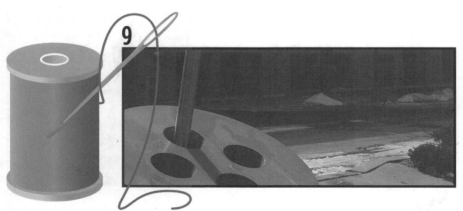

Just off of Broadway is this giant, of sorts,
Looks like it's propped up without supports.
A sculpture created by an artist named Dave,
Is found in the garment district—drive by and wave!

_____

10

Here are lions made of stone
Just sitting up there on their own.
Underneath a fancy valance.
(I hope that they don't lose their balance!)

11

Another day, another collar,
That's how Geo made his dollar
Back in the times when his style was cool.
Now, it's just lofts named after a jewel.

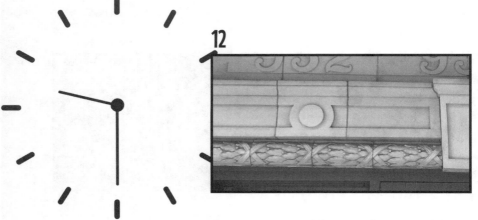

12

An entryway with carved stone trim,
Three addresses found within.
Hewn with details small and fine,
Don't look now—it's half past nine!

13

Stained glass flower windows so elegant and pretty, and
Adorning a steakhouse that every Kansas Citian
For 150 years knows at least medium-well,
Thanks to the name and the savory smell.

14

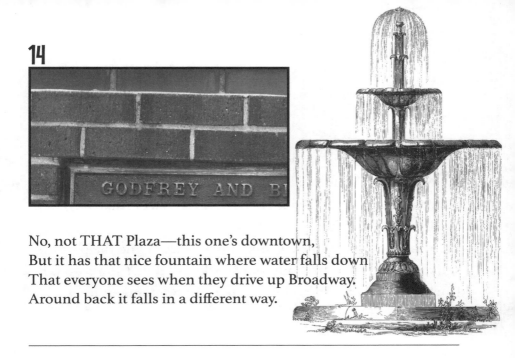

No, not THAT Plaza—this one's downtown,
But it has that nice fountain where water falls down
That everyone sees when they drive up Broadway.
Around back it falls in a different way.

15

This entrance presents as a wrought iron scroll,
Walk up this staircase and take a small stroll.
An archway leads to lofty spaces,
Come in and join all the happy faces.

MISSOURI
Harrisonville

When we say Harrisonville, we're talking about the city's historic square. Established in 1837, with pioneer traffic earlier than that, this is one of the oldest areas we visited. The buildings you'll see started going up in 1880. While the part we walked stretches over about four blocks, we didn't stray too far from the courthouse and found plenty to photograph for you.

1

This place has it all, from bath bombs to knickknacks;
You'll not want leave here empty-handed.
Shop 'til you drop, check all their stacks,
And the shaved ice is the best, to be candid.

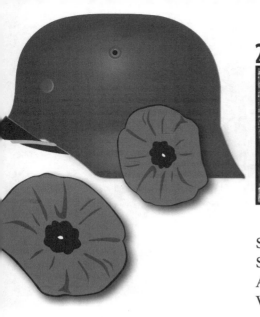

Standing at attention,
So proud and so tall,
A memorial to soldiers
Who gave our country their all.

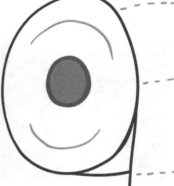

Stuck outside when nature calls and have a ladder handy?
This former hotel wall might be your modus operandi.
Sure, you'll need to bring a roll, it's open and it's drafty,
But when the going gets tough, you've got to get quite crafty.

4

A mural of war across the state border
When General Ewing issued his Order
And every farm outside of the town
Was evicted, then emptied, then burnt to the ground.

5

Stamped brightly in white
For all to see,
A declaration of love
For this community.

6

This mural shows Jennison's Jayhawker raid,
To which Quantrill responded and Ewing repaid.
They're shown here dressed in their uniform blues
And the infamous "Red Legs," a part of their shoes.

7

Head east a couple of blocks down Pearl,
Look to the left, and then enter a world
Where mayors and aldermen, planners and shapers,
Sign on the lines and shuffle their papers.

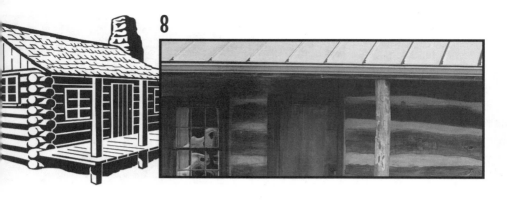

8

This Sharp little place right off of the square
Was built in the 1800s with care.
In the '70s they moved it to where it now rests
And for it they named an annual town fest.

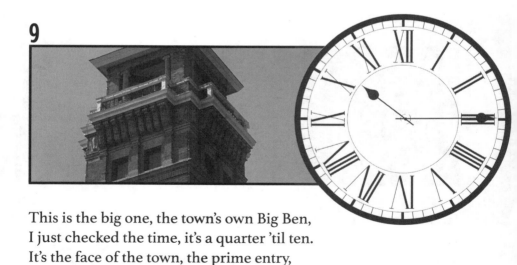

9

This is the big one, the town's own Big Ben,
I just checked the time, it's a quarter 'til ten.
It's the face of the town, the prime entry,
Look up where you are and you'll probably see.

10

This ain't yer Starbucks (though nothing's wrong with them).
But if you want something different, try this local gem.
They have so many flavors and even serve lunch,
You'll never go elsewhere, and that's not a hunch.

_____

_____

11

Since the 1970s, a specialized store,
A staple for cowboys and trainers galore.
Custom-made and built to last,
For those in this niche, this place is a blast.

_____

_____

12

The dancers dance to the fiddler's fiddle
On this charming square painted right in the middle
Of the front of a school where students display
Their poise and the grace of the art of ballet.

13

Order a steak, get it medium rare
In this cool little spot on the south of the square.
The Wall Street Deli in earlier years,
It's always remained a great place for beers.

14

Photographers with shared dreams opened this space.
Future brides, grooms, partiers? This is your place.
They will treat you like family on your special day,
Which is just what you want, and your event will SLAY.

15

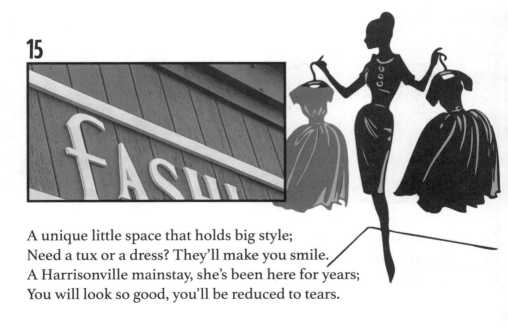

A unique little space that holds big style;
Need a tux or a dress? They'll make you smile.
A Harrisonville mainstay, she's been here for years;
You will look so good, you'll be reduced to tears.

Independence

Let us be the first to admit that this area got a little intense. You'll get your steps in, for sure, as you start near the courthouse and tromp all the way to the home of a former president. Luckily, you'll find plenty of places to rest, as well. This town was established in 1827 and has more history in it than we knew what to do with. If you find all these spots, you'll know as much as we do—then go read a book and tell us what you learn.

1

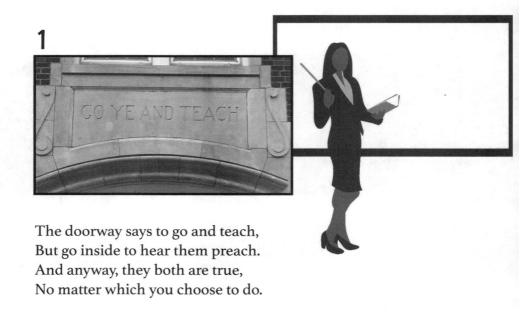

The doorway says to go and teach,
But go inside to hear them preach.
And anyway, they both are true,
No matter which you choose to do.

_____

_____

2

How about a frozen treat?
Here is where you go to eat.
If ice cream is for you a staple,
Find it here at Main and Maple.

3

You want to know what you can't do?
And what you can? This wall tells you.
And you can see a cherry fall
From ice cream painted on this wall.

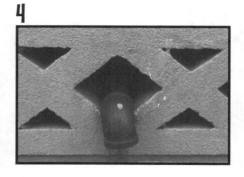

4

Next time that you walk about,
Try to find this downward spout.
They put it in a building's wall.
Does anything come out at all?

5

With concrete shutters and lots of trim,
Carl thinks they named it after him.
You can't see out or look inside.
It's just the perfect place to hide.

6

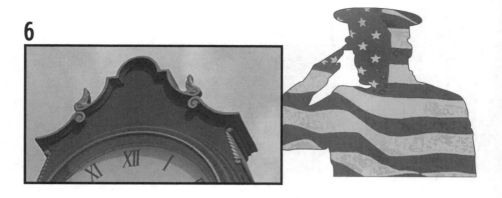

What has two faces and resides
Within a fence that is beside
A building built some years ago
To honor veterans, don't you know?

_____

_____

7

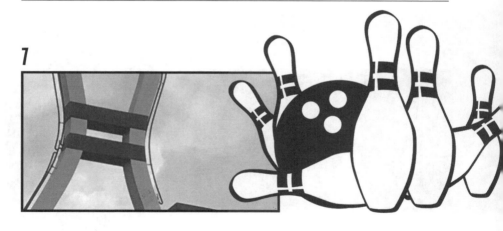

If one's on the roof and not in the rack,
I wonder where the other nine pins are at?
And what of the ball that knocks 'em down?
I don't think one big enough can be found.

_____

_____

8

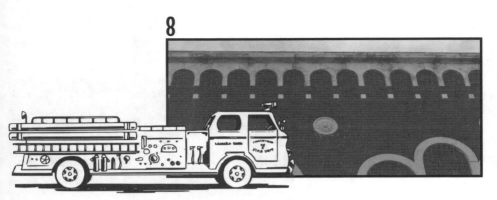

Windows decked in arches can be no mistake;
The roof's trimmed in white, like icing on a cake.
Where fire trucks used to answer the call,
This building now welcomes visitors and all.

9

The kings of old Egypt were ever so groovy,
So named after them is this place that shows movies.
That Art Deco signage right there on the square . . .
Go get your ticket and popcorn to share.

10

The most famous house in town
Is white with clapboard all around,
Covered with gingerbread that can't be eaten;
Respect for this home can't be beaten.

_____

_____

11

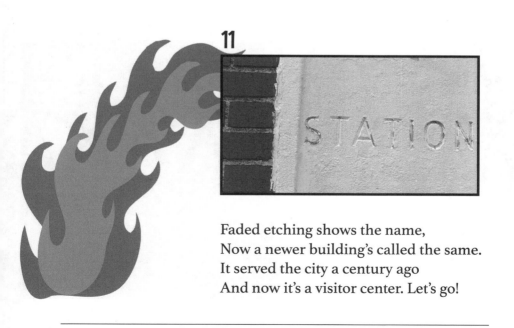

Faded etching shows the name,
Now a newer building's called the same.
It served the city a century ago
And now it's a visitor center. Let's go!

_____

_____

12

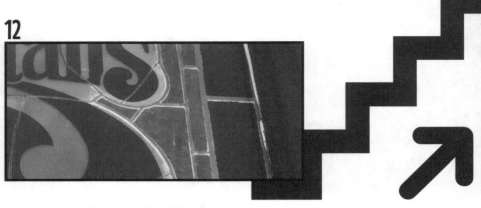

Look over a door and find beckoning
A mysterious sign causing reckoning.
It's bordered around the edges in black,
Made of some glass and lined with some cracks.

_____

_____

13

Find this fine scholar
As well as another
Where they once taught humanities
And still support the community.

_____

_____

14

He walked the streets here every day,
A "constitutional," he'd say.
And in this town they knew him well,
The president who gave 'em hell.

_____

_____

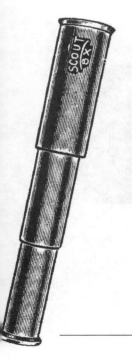

15

He guards the courthouse from his trusty steed,
A bronze-colored gift from Ol' Harry T.
With reins in his left hand and telescope in his right
He surveys the battlefield in case there's a fight.

_____

_____

16

ERECTED 1827

A first—and only—for 40 years long,
Built in 1827 and still standing strong.
No longer in service for what it was intended,
But now you can learn of its history so splendid.

17

In the heart of good old Independence Square
You'll find three wrought iron gates over there.
Walk through for a glass of wine and you'll see
A hundred or so locks, but not one key.

18

When you pass this monument,
Think of those whose lives were spent.
How they'd fight and how they'd fall—
All gave some, but some gave all.

_____

_____

19

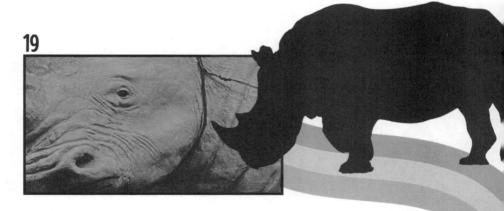

How much entertainment can one sign offer us?
A lot when it's this wacky, mounted rhinoceros
Right up on the brick wall with which he's bonded.
Where did his body go? Maybe he pawned it.

_____

_____

20

RET TRUMAN DANIEL.

Dignitaries come to Independence
To honor her most famous residents.
One year "Thirty-eight" stopped here,
As well as his First Daughter, his dear.

21

Drive your car right here and park it.
Then go shopping at this market.
You'll see the letters from afar;
They let you know right where you are.

22

In this frontier inn out west
Where travelers would get some rest,
Religious leaders spent some time
When Mormonism was a crime.

_____

_____

23

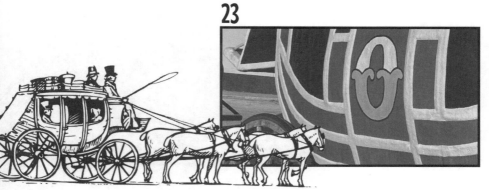

Here is a mystery you can unravel,
How can a stagecoach like this one travel?
Overland Park, for years was its home,
But then Independence is where it did roam.

_____

_____

MISSOURI

Lee's Summit

Beginning in 1865, this railroad town spent the first three years of its life as Strother. In 1868 it incorporated as Lee's Summit. Walk the business district near the Amtrak station, and you'll find a lot to do and see—at last count, over 100 locally owned businesses. In a regular year, this district draws hundreds of thousands of visitors, and the American Planning Association named it "America's Great Neighborhood" in 2019.

A horse and a carriage on this welcoming mural,
Painting of a town back when it was much more rural.
Walking too fast past this narrow rock alley,
You might totally miss out on this sweet little valley.

2

Finding this address twice only confuses,
But this building has had other uses.
Residents came here for documents
Before being used by its current occupants.

_____

_____

3

The building has had considerable restoration
Since its 1939 dedication.
Come learn about Lee's Summit heritage
Where people once bought their postage.

_____

_____

4

In the park by the station
Flies the flag of our nation,
A place for all to see,
Honoring those who kept us free.

5

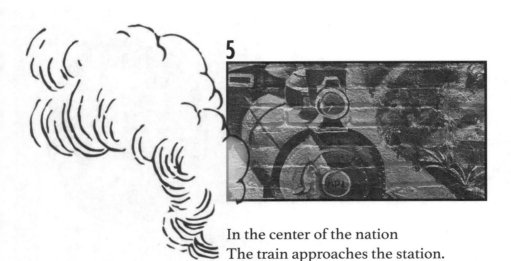

In the center of the nation
The train approaches the station.
In this old railroad town
Smoke bellows all around.

6

Lee's Summit's history
Is not without mystery.
The town's fabled outlaw son?
Or a law-abiding citizen?

7

This building on the main thoroughfare
Held many a business, such as hardware.
Where once you'd get a bike repaired,
You now can keep your money there.

8

Beneath a heart not far away
There is a pool where children play.
Frog and fish and laughter delights,
One of Lee's Summit's sweetest sights.

9

In the alley, you'll notice a sign
Letting you know where you are.
Are you uptown? No, you are not.
Quite the opposite, now, where is my car?

10

Who is SHE with her fiery hair?
Her nails so bright and her skin so fair?
What is she thinking behind those cool shades?
In this alleyway, she's got mystery in spades.

_____

_____

11

You can buy a bike and then go next door
And make your hair look better,
Then cross the street and have a drink
Where a finger points with a letter.

_____

_____

12

A Grammy-winning jazz musician,
Local talent with worldwide fame!
This sign is a small tribute to a man
Not just any city can claim.

_____

_____

13

Free concerts by the old depot,
Memorial, fountain, and more.
A lot of sweet green space for the peep-o,
Look around to see what's in store.

_____

_____

14

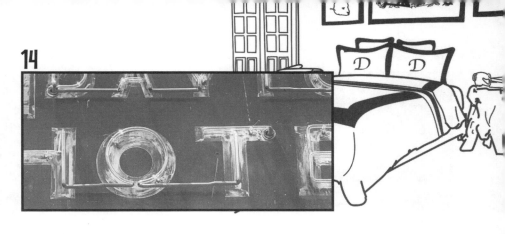

A hospital in the 1900s first,
And then a hotel, no more people were nursed.
Now, all that is left is a sign to see,
A private residence; another layer for its history.

_____

_____

15

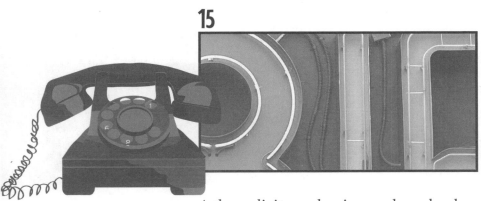

A three-digit number in purple and red,
You'll dial them first in this city.
Add them together and it is to be seen:
The sum of the numbers will equal fifteen.

_____

_____

16

Back nearly 100 years ago,
This shop kept every car on the go.
Now it's named for a legume variety
But best known for wings and that fab BLT.

17

Chugga-chugga, choo-choo
Doesn't run, but that's cool.
You can always visit it whenever,
because it's now parked here forever.

18

What began in St. Louis in 1975,
Isn't a typical bar, pub, or dive.
From traditional Irish Scot food and smiles,
This place is just like the real British Isles.

_____

_____

19

Buskers, go ahead and leave your instruments at home;
Use this city's resident drum and xylophone.
Gather your friends, clap your hands, stomp your feet,
Make some music to liven up this Lee's Summit street.

_____

_____

Parkville

This town is named for George S. Park, not the parklike setting of this riparian area. George was an entrepreneur and Army colonel and was rumored to have survived a firing line (see story in *Secret Kansas City*). Parkville became an official town in 1844, and is now home to a university, a charming downtown, a lot of art, and many green spaces.

1

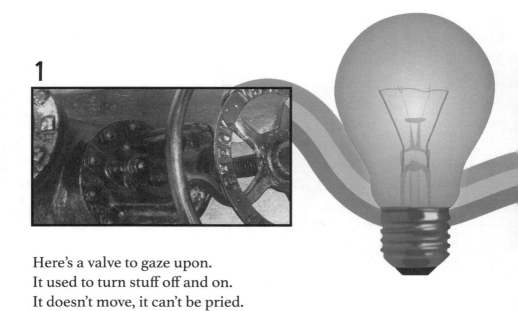

Here's a valve to gaze upon.
It used to turn stuff off and on.
It doesn't move, it can't be pried.
But what would happen if you tried?

_____

_____

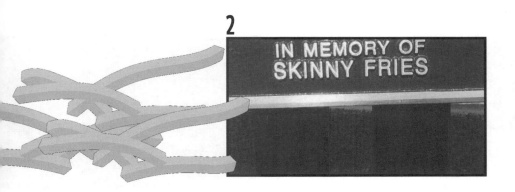

2

Under the eaves and above the trenches,
You're likely to find a lot of benches.
Most have nothing on the back,
But this one has a lovely plaque.

3

There's a bench made for one
By a walk that is gray,
Where a cat sleeps below
And a dog looks away.

4

If you're hoping to
Watch bluebirds fly,
Find these on a wall
'Cause they don't need the sky.

_____

_____

5

There are black double doors
Between lights you can see
And a stained glass window
Where a transom really ought to be.

_____

_____

6

Jack from old Parkville, that lifelong resident,
Loved his town dearly and was never hesitant
To build all the bridges and fix every crack;
They remember him fondly with this lovely plaque.

_____

_____

7

Every shop has one for access,
But not like this—it's one of the best.
Wear your mittens when it is ice-cold,
Then step right in over the threshold.

_____

_____

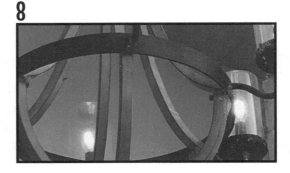

8

What typically lights up inside,
Illuminates the way outside.
In black and white, it recreates
A time and place to celebrate.

9

Where flowing water does not churn,
There is a wheel that does not turn.
It serves to set a pretty scene
Down by the old mill stream.

10

It's long and traffic-light yellow,
Well-used and kinda mellow.
And while it no longer goes,
It's best if you stay on your toes.

11

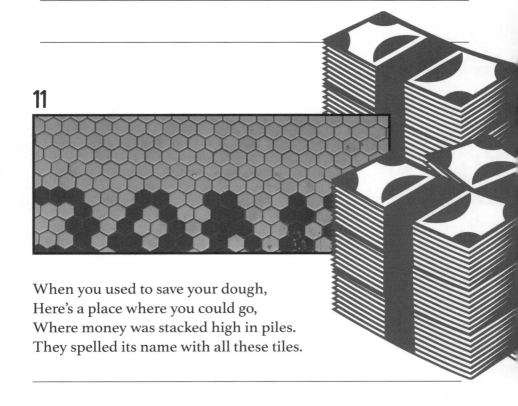

When you used to save your dough,
Here's a place where you could go,
Where money was stacked high in piles.
They spelled its name with all these tiles.

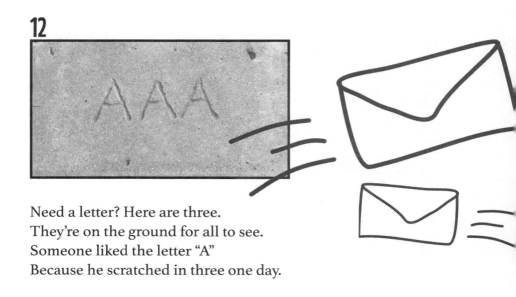

12

Need a letter? Here are three.
They're on the ground for all to see.
Someone liked the letter "A"
Because he scratched in three one day.

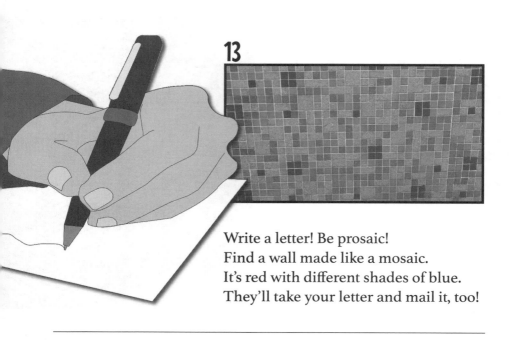

13

Write a letter! Be prosaic!
Find a wall made like a mosaic.
It's red with different shades of blue.
They'll take your letter and mail it, too!

14

If you go out for a run,
Pass by building Number 1.
Don't go in to get a view.
It's their job to come to you.

15

You've heard the name and know the story
About the man and all his glory,
But in the town there was no joy;
Tough luck for Mudville's favorite boy.

16

Is it a plant growing?
Is it a fire glowing?
Up from the ground
Where folks hike around.

_____

_____

17

Here's to a man who spoke and wrote
And piloted a riverboat.
He's lounging on a bench in town,
And you can join him! Go sit down!

_____

_____

18

The harness racer's horse is going
Straight to where the wind is blowing.
You'll need to look up in the sky
Because he's mounted way up high.

_____

_____

19

The "prince" of this city will toast
You from his Pocket Park post.
A man of many nicknames, they say,
In every season, it's a beautiful day.

_____

_____

Waldo

Waldo is named for David Waldo, who bought 1,000 acres of Jackson County land in 1841. Kansas City annexed Waldo in 1909, but many locals still think of it as its own city. We spent time at about 75th Street and Wornall Road, an area that's pretty high-traffic—it's full of stuff to see and do, but not as walkable as some other neighborhoods.

1

The neighborhood's nickname appears up high
In blue and white for passersby,
And if you keep walking down the street,
There's another WET place where people meet.

_____

_____

2

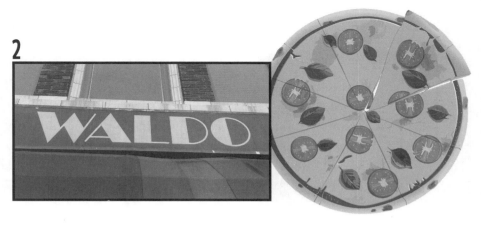

Indulge if you will, a bit of rhymin'
About the time a St. Louis pieman
Offered a slice with a neighborhood name
And scattered out cards from a trivia game.

3

Well, that was fun,
Wouldn't you say?
To party on a rooftop . . .
Doesn't happen every day.

4

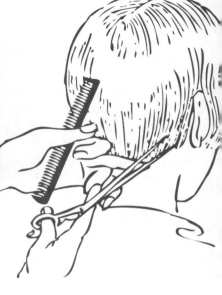

After you've fueled up, stop
At a business next door that's topped
By a shady and colorful striped awning
For a trim that won't leave you yawning.

_____

_____

5

Look up for a balcony so dinky,
Beneath is Japanese for using ink(y).
Come inside to get your bod decorated;
What's your choice? It doesn't have to be G-rated.

_____

_____

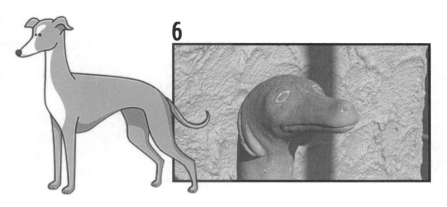

6

Silent as a stone as I sit here all alone,
Waiting for a passerby or two.
Some step in closer and stay for awhile;
Others pause for a second to flash me a smile.

_____

_____

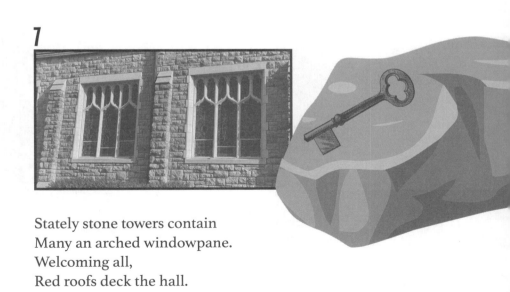

7

Stately stone towers contain
Many an arched windowpane.
Welcoming all,
Red roofs deck the hall.

_____

_____

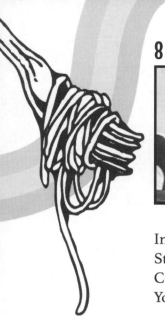

8

In il centro of Waldo,
Stop in for a bite.
Comfort food and desserts—
Your pantalones will leave tight.

9

Huge heart for others here below,
Working with an org named ZERO.
Got a smile for girls and boys,
Pink hibiscus love and joy.

10

On the corner by a STOP,
Spot the hydrant. Can you park? You canNOT.
Corrugated walls look so legit;
Now you've got it.

_____

_____

11

Look up for a flame
Above a place name.
Keep walking and looking;
This sign means good cooking.

_____

_____

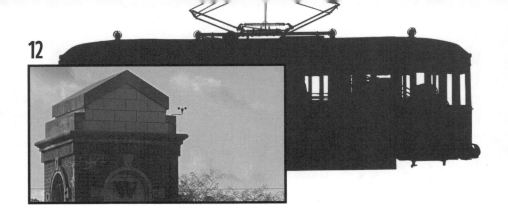

12

Near the Trolley Track Trail,
Following a path that once was a rail,
Stands a monument tall.
One word that says it all.

_____

_____

13

One of many places to live
To enjoy all the neighborhood has to give,
Trolley Trail Shops, a local spot.
Come see all that Waldo's got!

_____

_____

Close your eyes and follow your nose;
And don't let a car hit your toes.
What was originally called Patsy's,
This Kansas City treat is anything but nasty.

_____

_____

Westport

Westport is another part of town so packed with history that you're sure to have missed it as a casual bar-hopper. Its founding dates to about 1833, when it was a trading post and the westernmost spot for travelers to resupply. Eventually the Santa Fe, Oregon, and California trails all followed Westport Road. The area was annexed by Kansas City in 1899. You've got a lot to look for here.

1

His murder was a tipping point in 2020,
But his was not the only one; there have been plenty.
We'll have heightened awareness from this time hence,
Thankful, we now agree: silence is violence.

2

ALL DISTANCES. EVERYONE

These words read about feet that run,
A bright message found under the sun.
Fast or slow, the capped words are clear;
Keep your eyes alert, because you are near.

3

The painter paints as the horses trot.
The color is faint above the city lot.
A girl, two women, and a dog standing by,
About to get trampled if the horses can't fly.

4

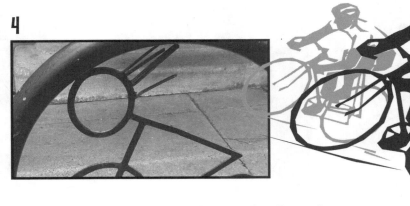

No helmet is needed, cause she's made of metal;
Ain't got no feet, ain't got no pedal,
No motion at all, she stuck in one place,
A tribute to cyclists (but one with no face).

5

This building once held slaves, so the rumor goes,
Grim history, if true, but no one really knows.
But in recent times, for more years than not,
If you want to party, then this is the spot.

6

Bob Berdella aside (let's not mention him again),
This is the place for finds simple or arcane.
It's acres of stuff you just can't find in malls.
If you have time to spare, come wander these halls.

_____

_____

7

THE FRENCH AN

For 200 years, this trail's history
Got lots of press, so it's no mystery.
But this wordy signage dives deep in the past;
These stories will leave you amazed and aghast!

_____

_____

8

We're a beer kind of town, maybe kinda shy,
Just casual and laid back, I can't say why.
Find this guitar dude sporting his hat;
He's jamming for fun, his fingers are fat.

9

A staring lion seems to ask from this sign,
"Did you forget the erection of 1899?"
Stationed right near a swanky new bar,
From that thought he never strays far.

10

Our young hero passes with all he's got,
He's huge and red on the side of this spot.
His face you've seen on billboards and screen;
You know him best as Number 15.

_____

_____

11

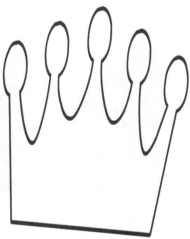

Honestly, weren't we all Raised Royal?
Even in years their efforts were foiled?
We still paint murals to honor the men
Who we anxiously wait to see play again.

_____

_____

12

What is the madness in this depiction
Of a scene I hope is purely fiction?
You can either defend yourself or hide;
If you want to karate chop, go inside.

13

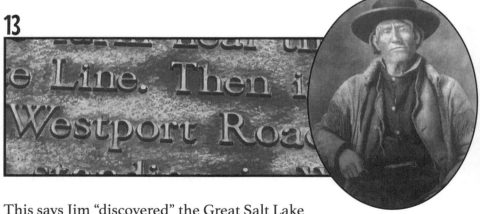

This says Jim "discovered" the Great Salt Lake
And a pass through the Rockies to survive you should take.
Oh, great, he was also an "Indian fighter,"
And he sits here with dudes who couldn't be whiter.

14

Here's a map you've often missed,
Showing three trails west—you get the gist.
On its traffic island, it's tough to access,
When you cross to see it, don't cause a mess!

_____

_____

15

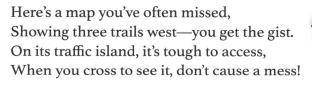

Along the trail, the DAR traveled the nation,
Placing markers like this about "civilization."
This was the Harris House, now it's a bar;
Civilization hasn't made it too far.

_____

_____

16

It's been on this street since Dr. Who.
If you'd lived long ago, you'd have known what to do.
Now it can keep you out of the rain,
But as far as comms goes, there's nothing to gain.

_____

_____

17

Remember 1839, we didn't know our name?
For 4,220 bucks the area was claimed.
We're the City of Kansas, according to this seal.
If we'd have been Possum Trot, how would you feel?

_____

_____

18

Here they sit on a traffic island,
The freighter, surveyor, and mountain man.
Formally dedicated in 1987,
Now all these dudes are up in heaven.

_____

_____